Cambridge Elements ≡

Elements in Histories of Emotions and the Senses
edited by
Jan Plamper
Goldsmiths, University of London

PLAYFUL VIRTUAL VIOLENCE

An Ethnography of Emotional Practices in Video Games

Christoph Bareither
Humboldt University of Berlin

CAMBRIDGE
UNIVERSITY PRESS

University Printing House, Cambridge CB2 8BS, United Kingdom

One Liberty Plaza, 20th Floor, New York, NY 10006, USA

477 Williamstown Road, Port Melbourne, VIC 3207, Australia

314–321, 3rd Floor, Plot 3, Splendor Forum, Jasola District Centre,
New Delhi – 110025, India

79 Anson Road, #06–04/06, Singapore 079906

Cambridge University Press is part of the University of Cambridge.

It furthers the University's mission by disseminating knowledge in the pursuit of
education, learning, and research at the highest international levels of excellence.

www.cambridge.org
Information on this title: www.cambridge.org/9781108819435
DOI: 10.1017/9781108873079

When citing this work, please include a reference to the DOI 10.1017/9781108873079

First published 2020

A catalogue record for this publication is available from the British Library.

ISBN 978-1-108-81943-5 Paperback
ISSN 2632-1068 (online)
ISSN 2632-105X (print)

Playful Virtual Violence

An Ethnography of Emotional Practices in Video Games

Elements in Histories of Emotions and the Senses

DOI: 10.1017/9781108873079
First published online: October 2020

Christoph Bareither
Humboldt University of Berlin

Author for correspondence: Christoph Bareither,
christoph.bareither@hu-berlin.de

Abstract: Violence in video games has been a controversial object of public discourse for several decades. However, the question of what kind of emotional experiences players enact when playing with representations of physical violence in games has been largely ignored. Building upon an extensive ethnographic study of players' emotional practices in video games, including participant observation in online games, qualitative interviews, and an analysis of YouTube videos and gaming magazines since the 1980s, this Element provides new insights into the complexity and diversity of player experiences and the pleasures of playful virtual violence. Instead of either defending or condemning the players, it contributes foundational, unprejudiced knowledge for a societal and academic debate on a critical aspect of video gaming.

This title is also available as Open Access on Cambridge Core.
Keywords: violence, games, emotions, digital media, ethnography

Isbns: 9781108819435 (PB), 9781108873079 (OC)
Issns: 2632-1068 (online), 2632-105X (print)

Contents

Introduction

'Hey!' a masked guard yells, pointing at Lara Croft, who has been surreptitiously moving through an enemy bunker. 'Oh shit', Sarazar, the player controlling Lara, utters. Just as the guard begins to shoot, Lara dispatches him with an arrow from her compound bow. It's too late though. 'Our cover's been blown . . . ', Sarazar concedes, as throngs of computer-controlled enemies open fire. He notices a fuel drum nearby and with a 'Come on!' coaxes one of Lara's arrows towards the target, causing a loud explosion that sends a guard flying back. 'Bam!' Sarazar exclaims. Now the battle is in full swing. Lara takes cover from Molotov cocktails and launches an arrow into an adversary's stomach. 'How do you like that?!' Sarazar cries, taunting the dying enemy before ducking under a hail of bullets. 'You bastards!' he intones earnestly as Lara Croft picks off several more enemies in quick succession, earning an additional skill point. But just then, a Molotov cocktail strikes her and explodes. Splatters of blood appear on the edges of the screen and Lara groans in pain. Sarazar seems to suffer vicariously. 'Oww!' The enemies pick up their attacks. Sarazar swaps Lara's bow for a shotgun loaded with incendiary shells. 'Bam!' Sarazar cries out, as one approaching enemy is thrown backwards, engulfed in flames, and another falls to ground. 'How's that feel? Scumbag!' For every enemy killed another seems to take his place and Sarazar becomes nervous. 'Oh god, how many are there?' He decides to retreat, nimbly steering Lara through the falling debris. From the rear position she takes down enemies one by one. In the absence of a direct kill, targeted immobilisation will do. 'Nut shot!' When the last enemy falls after being struck by a climbing axe in hand-to-hand combat, Sarazar is hungry for more. 'Was that it?' he asks, while Lara elegantly slides down a rope into the courtyard below. He notices that one enemy soldier, large and heavily armoured, is still alive. The opponent rises up and yells, 'You will die!' 'We'll see about that, big boy', Sarazar responds. Neither sword nor shotgun shell can penetrate the opponent's full-length shield. Lara elegantly sidesteps a strike and, with the enemy's flank now exposed, fires a blast into his body, causing him to collapse and burst into flame. Sarazar lets out a satisfied 'Ha!' He proceeds to collect items from several dead soldiers, includ-ing parts for more powerful weapons. 'Come on, hand over your stuff', he says, and then sums up his impression of the level so far: 'That was a crazy battle! What a way to start the episode'.

The action I have just described is from a Let's Play video of the 2013 video game *Tomb Raider*.[1] Let's Play videos, in which gamers document the

---

[1] Sarazar (30 March 2013). Let's Play Tomb Raider #029 – Gefecht in der Ruine [Full-HD] [German]. Online video clip. 1:17–4:50. www.youtube.com/embed/LKqkrCEwuXE? start=77&end=290

playthrough of video games, have been an extremely popular YouTube genre for some time, and Sarazar is one of the scene's biggest stars in Germany. With over 120,000 views, the episode is about average for his videos. The clip I describe above illustrates a key observation of this Element: violence in video games – inflecting it, the effects produced by it, the experience of one's own ability, the feeling of domination, the rewards in the form of points, the threat and tension, the stress and 'pain' – can be a source of great pleasure for gamers, and not just a few. Millions of players around the world play violent video games every day.

The pleasure they feel is by no means new. Since the beginning of the 1980s, when video games migrated from arcades into living rooms, action games have been a popular genre in the gaming world. As graphics evolved over the next three decades, players moved from shooting at abstract pixels to increasingly detailed representations of human bodies. The realistic depictions of violence made possible by new graphics technology set off heated public debates around the world, with many attributing mass shootings to experience with violent first-person shooter games. A plethora of scholarly articles and books have since emerged purporting to show the deleterious effects of video game violence. While a comprehensive review of those works lies beyond the scope of this Element, it suffices to point out that precious few of their authors have thought to ask what makes violent video games so pleasurable for their millions of fans. In this Element, I provide answers to that question and in doing so help close a conspicuous gap in the literature.

At first blush, the question *why* so many people take pleasure in video game violence seems nearly impossible to answer: the biological dispositions of players are too complex, their socio-cultural surroundings, too heterogeneous, and their tastes, too individual to allow anything like a universal explanation. Yet the fact that millions of people play violent video games suggests a clear link between violence and pleasure. Instead of asking *why* so many people take pleasure in virtual violence, my work focuses on *how*, specifically: How do players emotionally experience video game violence?

To answer this question, the study does not enter the well-trodden territory of media psychology. Nor does it offer an extensive review of game theory scholarship. Readers interested in these aspects might consult Gareth Schott's *Violent Games* (2016), which considers violence in video games through the prism of both game theory and media psychology. While the book provides many interesting insights, Rune Klevjer observes in his review that Schott's analysis uses 'theory as a blank check to be able to universally proclaim that violence in games is not an issue, and that anyone concerned with its impact in society and culture, whether parents or regulators, are led astray by a total misconception' (2018). Klevjer rejects Schott's underlying assumption, arguing that 'violence *is* important to the DNA of gaming' (2018).

I could not agree Klevjer more. Indeed, my main objective is to show that an ethnography of emotions can help us understand everyday gaming practices while shedding light on how violence comes to be a key factor in the popularity of video games. I neither defend nor condemn the pleasure players take in video game violence. I observe how people experience virtual violence and how they articulate their emotions in the process. From these observations, I then draw conclusions regarding the characteristics of the emotional experiences. Like most ethnographers, I eschew reductions of complex phenomena in favour of nuanced examinations of people's actual emotional experiences. In this regard, the study is less representative than explorative, considering the many facets of pleasure in video game violence through an ethnographic lens.

The research for this study took place primarily in Germany, where debates about violent video games have been especially heated given the country's history and its strong response to anything that might seem to celebrate violence. This makes Germany somewhat unique, but also a unique opportunity to explore the questions posed here.

The majority of the interviews, videos, and texts cited in this study are originally in German. The English translation has attempted to render the colloquial style of the gamers' language and jargon. Some of the references and cited literature are available only in German and have been translated to make them accessible for international audiences.[2] Unlike my *Gewalt im Computerspiel* (2016), which dwells at length on previous scholarship and empirical examples, this work focuses on core insights, inviting readers to dive into the video game experience more or less directly. Those interested in delving into the literature on emotions in gaming or on the ethnography of video games more generally should refer to my *Gewalt im Computerspiel*.

This Element draws extensively on materials that are freely accessible online, most notably articles from video game magazines (1983–2014) and Let's Play videos on YouTube. Readers of the digital text can use the hyperlinks in the footnotes to access these resources. The 'recommended example' links feature videos that exemplify the phenomena under discussion. Although the videos are all in German, they nevertheless offer a rich audio-visual impression of gaming behaviours.

The Element begins with Section 1 on key concepts and theories before turning to questions of methodology in Section 2. Sections 3 to 6 explore the

---

[2] All translations are my responsibility and were made in collaboration with Wesley Merkes, Philip Saunders and Dominic Bonfliglio, who translated and edited parts of my *Gewalt im Computerspiel* (2016).

different emotional experiences with virtual violence of video games. The final Section situates the preceding analysis in a broader academic and societal context.

1 Emotional Practices, Popular Pleasures, and Virtual Violence

John Fiske, in his influential work *Understanding Popular Culture*, writes, 'Popular pleasure exists only in its practices, contexts, and moments of production' (Fiske 1989, 50). Fiske's view paved the way for later ethnographic studies that approached pleasure as a product not of passive consumption but of active practice (Maase 2019, 90–5). I share Fisk's perspective, but I also go beyond it. I understand the practices that give rise to pleasure to be *emotional practices* that produce pleasurable emotions. The specific idea of emotional practices has grown out of the work of cultural anthropologist Monique Scheer (2012, 2016, forthcoming) who argues that emotions are not passive and internal but woven into everyday cultural practices that shape and produce them:

> Though emotions may sometimes be experienced as if they happen to us, they are always something our bodies do, and do them according to patterns structured by factors such as language, social order, and local styles, and they are embedded in larger sets of cultural practices. Understanding emotions as actions of mind and body means that they are not epiphenomena of people's activities but linked with other doings and sayings involving certain spaces, objects, sounds, and other people. It is useful to think about emotions with practice theory, I believe, since it provides a concept of action, of 'doing', that can encompass intentional, deliberate action, but includes, and indeed stresses, habituated behavior executed without much cognitive attention paid. (forthcoming)

It is important to distinguish here between 'emotions-as-practices' and 'emotional practices'. On the one hand, emotions-as-practices are practices that bodies do; on the other, emotions are embedded in larger culturally determined emotional practices for handling feelings in everyday life. The latter mobilise, articulate, name, and regulate emotions-as-practices. Scheer (2016) identifies different types of emotional practices, including religious practices, such as prayer; social practices, such as wooing romantic partners; and pop-culture practices, such as playing video games. Her theory does not aim to dismiss other concepts of emotion or affect but to give ethnographers a new way of understanding particular social phenomena. 'If we think of emotions not as something we have, but as something we do', Scheer writes, 'then we can examine them the same way we examine any other sort of culturally shaped behaviour that serves the purpose of communicating, interacting, relating to other people and things' (Scheer forthcoming).

What Scheer says about emotions also applies to pleasure. The interconnected web of practices that constitute pleasure is composed largely of emotional practices that mobilise, shape, and articulate feelings. And all emotional practices are built on practical – which is to say, embodied – knowledge. Pierre Bourdieu's practice theory – alluded to in the block quote from Scheer – is central here, particularly his notion of habitus, which, for all the criticism it has received, usefully describes the idea of an 'embodied knowledge' that guides, and is permanently shaped by, everyday practices (Scheer 2012, 199–209). In the same sense, emotional practices shape, and are guided by, embodied knowledge that evokes, refuses, or enables particular ways of feeling.

Because emotional practices articulate embodied knowledge, they provide a good starting point for the ethnographic examination of pleasure. A particularly rich example of this is everyday language. The investigation of linguistic representations has been a central pillar of the ethnographic study of emotion ever since Catherine Lutz's (1988) *Unnatural Emotions* and *Language and the Politics of Emotion*, which she co-edited with Lila Abu-Lughod (1990b). Lutz and Abu-Lughod understand language as an emotional practice: 'Emotion can be said to be created in, rather than shaped by, speech in the sense that it is postulated as an entity in language where its meaning to social actors is also elaborated' (Abu-Lughod & Lutz 1990a, 12). Donald Brenneis, in his article for the same volume, echoes the idea: 'Language is about something, does something, and is something itself; the content and conduct of emotional communication are integrally related' (Brenneis 1990, 114). William Reddy elucidates the idea in his work on the history of emotions (1997; 2001, 96–110). He argues that linguistic utterances do not merely describe emotions but actively shape and intensify them. Borrowing from performance theory, he terms such speech acts 'emotives' (Reddy 2001, 105). Emotives make up a crucial part of the emotional practices I examine in this Element.

An ongoing question in work on emotional practices is whether individual emotions are analytically distinguishable. Most ethnographic approaches in the study of emotion reject the idea of reducing certain practices to discrete basic emotions like those identified by Paul Ekman (1972). However, the question whether individual emotions can be differentiated at all remains unsettled among ethnographers. For the study of pleasure, at least, the approach of the philosopher Robert C. Solomon (2007) offers some help. Showing certain parallels to the theory of emotional practices (see Scheer 2012, 194), Solomon introduces the idea of 'emotional experience', which he defines as 'a complex of many experiences; sensations; various ways of being aware of the world, our own bodies, and intentions; and also thoughts and reflections on our emotions, all melded together in what is typically encountered as a single more or less unified experience' (2007, 244). Thinking of emotions as part of rich emotional experiences allows a more nuanced analysis of pleasure, one that, instead of attempting to create an exhaustive categorisation of the emotions that constitute pleasure, seeks to understand their diversity, complexity, relationality, and individual significance.

Experiences, in this sense, can neither be reduced to acquired knowledge nor to accumulated sensory perceptions. Rather, as John Dewey argued in *Art as Experience* (1980(1934)), they are active processes that interweave perceptions, interpretations, and actions (Maase 2019, 83–6). 'Experience', Dewey (1980) writes, 'is the result, the sign, and the reward of that interaction of organism and environment which, when it is carried to the full, is a transformation of interaction into participation and communication' (p. 22). From the perspective of practice theory one can go further and argue that experience does not exist outside of practice. German idiom already expresses this idea: one 'makes' an experience (*Erfahrung machen*) rather than 'having' one. To convey in English the constructedness of experience, I have borrowed from practice theory and speak of *enacting* emotional experiences.

Playful Virtual Violence

This Element looks at practices of emotional experiences with regard to a phenomenon that I call 'playful virtual violence'. Aside from a few notable exceptions, virtual violence and video game violence are rarely discussed explicitly in the literature. Andreas Jahn-Sudmann and Arne Schröder (2010) offer a useful starting point with their concept of 'ludic violence', which they argue has a 'similarity relationship' to physical violence (p. 133). While this partly gets at what I mean by playful virtual violence, my concept requires additional unpacking. It makes sense to start from the end and work backwards. 'Violence' can mean very different things. It can be physical, psychic, structural, symbolic, cultural, political, direct, personal, individual, or collective. I use 'violence' explicitly in the sense of physical violence, which Merriam-Webster defines as 'the use of physical force so as to injure, abuse, damage, or destroy'. Using 'violence' strictly in this sense has a number of advantages. First, physical violence, as Randall Collins (2008) notes, 'has a clear core referent, which we can study using micro-situational observations' (p. 24). This means that, in contrast to other forms of violence, such as symbolic or structural violence, physical violence is easily recognisable and empirically observable, though the intent to harm is not always apparent. Second, its observability enables analytical and ethnographic understanding without resorting to normative judgements. This is especially critical when approaching a topic as controversial as video game violence.

Of course, physical violence in video games is different from actual physical violence, for the violence it depicts is virtual. In his influential ethnographic study *Second Life*, Tom Boellstorff (2018) argued that the 'virtual' should not be thought of in opposition to the 'real' but rather in relation to the 'actual':

> The Oxford English Dictionary defines 'virtual' as a reference to something that exists in essence or effect, although not formally or actually. Virtuality can thus be understood in terms of potentiality; it can be said to exist whenever there is a perceived gap between experience and 'the actual'. This is now the most important meaning of 'virtual' with regards to virtual worlds; 'virtual' connotes approaching the actual *without arriving there*. (p. 19)

The philosopher Philip Brey (2014) goes one further and distinguishes between 'digital objects' and 'virtual objects'. Digital objects are the bits and bytes calculated by the computer. Though digital objects lack identifiable mass and an explicit location in physical space, Brey maintains that they are nevertheless persistent, uniform, and stable structures with specifiable relations to the hardware, and hence can claim the status of objects. By contrast, virtual objects are generated on top of digital objects, as it were. They are 'digital objects that appear to us as physical objects and that we interact with in a manner similar to physical objects' (Brey 2014, 44). Crucially, virtual objects appear not identical but similar to physical objects. For a digital object to become a virtual object, a human agent must recognise the virtual object's similarity to an actual object and then do something with it. In his seminal work *Umgang mit Technik* ('Interacting with technology'), the cultural anthropologist Stefan Beck (1997) argues that only when human agents use a technology to some end does it become a socioculturally relevant *Tat-Sache*, a play on words emphasising the interdependency of fact (*Tatsache*), action (*Tat*), and thing (*Sache*) (p. 353). From an ethnographic perspective, what technology is matters less than how it is put into practice. Rather than regarding the virtual as a self-contained ontological state, it makes more sense to think of the virtual as a set of practices that enact similarities between virtual entities (e.g., objects, spaces, bodies, sounds, movements) and their physical counterparts.

The final term to unpack is 'playful'. Like violence, play admits a multitude of meanings, and a variety of very different concepts exist in video-game scholarship. My understanding of play is bound up with its relationship to seriousness and draws on the work of Gregory Bateson (2006), who examined the relationship in his 1954 lecture 'A Theory of Play and Fantasy'. For Bateson, play belongs to a theory of communication involving different levels of abstraction when signalling messages. He famously came up with the idea while observing monkeys at the San Francisco Zoo. In the primate house, he noticed two monkeys engaged in play fighting, going through the motions of a real physical altercation but without using serious force. In their playful wrangling, Bateson believed he saw a form of metacommunication with a specific message: 'This is play', which is to say, 'These actions, in which we now engage, do not denote what would be denoted by those actions which these actions denote'. 'The playful nip denotes the bite', Bateson explains, 'but it does not denote what would be denoted by the bite' (p. 317). The metacommunicative message 'this is play' is a paradoxical message, for play signifies a handling of particular meanings distinct from non-play yet necessarily constituted by it. Though play is not serious, it is only possible in reference to the serious. Bateson elucidates the relationship by way of an analogy. Just as maps are systems of reference to a territory, games are a network of references to non-playful meanings (p. 317). For Bateson, the relationship between map and territory, or between playful reference to a non-playful signal and the non-playful signal itself, are neither clearly the same nor clearly distinct. Rather, 'in play, they are both equated and discriminated' (Bateson 2006, 321). Britta Neitzel succinctly summarises Bateson's argument: 'A playful action denotes, and at the same time it does not denote, the "real" action to which it refers' (Neitzel 2008, 281).

The relationship between play and non-play gives rise to the distinctive function of play as a process of emotional experience. The experience of pleasure fits well into the model, though Bateson touches on the subject only in passing. Understanding pleasure as a playful activity means focusing on how those at play enact enjoyable emotional experiences through playful reference to non-playful actions. Playful violence is reference by means of verbal and non-verbal signals to actual physical violence within a process framed through metacommunication as *play*. In this sense, Bateson's fighting monkeys are engaging in playful violence, as are children playing cops and robbers. In video games, the practice is inflected by digital technology to become playful *virtual* violence. Through the similarity between actual physical violence and its digital representations, gamers generate a rich tapestry of emotional experiences. The task of this Element is to explore those experiences in all their variety.

2 Studying Emotional Practices in Video Games

What is the best way to study emotional practices and the emotional experiences they enact in video games? I settled on four main methods: (1) participant observation online and offline, (2) qualitative interviews, (3) the analysis of

Let's Play videos, and (4) the analysis of video gaming magazine articles from 1983 to 2014.

Throughout the study, I triangulate the data to arrive at different perspectives for each area of investigation. In employing a variety of research methods, I was able to collect different kinds of data, which, instead of treating discretely, I set in relation to allow for a richer understanding and offset possible blind spots with individual approaches. This is crucial because emotional experiences, by their very nature, escape precise definition and measurement. Accordingly, I do not aim to codify specific emotions but to circle around multiple forms of practice and the spheres of experience associated with them.

My main method was participant observation, which generates insights through interactive presence in the research field (Boellstorff et al. 2012). I focused my efforts on the emotional practices and experiences of individuals who regularly played online multiplayer games. I observed and noted what players did within a game and what they said over audio channels. I also followed participants as they interacted with online gamer groups via headset, a very common practice. The emotional practices central to this study were composed of verbal (and occasionally written) statements about events in the game. Players provided running commentary on the gameplay – rejoicing, showing annoyance or anger, bragging, laughing, praising their friends, describing their experiences, and so on. Hence, my observation encompassed not only the actions of the players in the games but also their communication and the relationship between the two.

I recorded my observations in a digital field journal that I ran on a second laptop next to the gaming PC. The groups studied were predominantly male and mostly composed of players between the ages of sixteen and forty. Observation time totalled around 1,200 hours and was spread across the online shooters *DayZ, Counter-Strike*, and *Battlefield* (each in different versions), the massively multiplayer online role-playing game (MMORPG) *The Elder Scrolls Online*, and a number of other games. At the time of the study, all the games were in the mainstream of online multiplayer games, each with hundreds of thousands of regular users.

I supplemented the online participant observation by visiting two local area network (LAN) parties. LAN parties are events where large number of players – the ones I saw had between 300 and 600 attendees – come together for several days in order to take part in competitive video gaming. These offered a productive field for observing the competitive dimensions of playful virtual violence.

I interviewed thirty-seven players, some individually and some in groups, about their everyday gaming life. I conducted a total of sixteen interviews with an average length of 83 minutes (around 33 hours in total). All interviews were conducted via online voice chat in order to offer participants a certain degree of anonymity given the sensitive nature of the topic. (I never asked the interviewees for their real names.) The purpose was to better understand the players' emotional experiences while playing video games. I did not seek to describe the interior experiences of the participants or look for 'authentic emotions'. Rather, I used the interviews to contextualise the emotional practices observed in the field. In selecting the participants, I refrained from applying a predetermined criterion such as age or sex. More important was that they were open to having frank discussions about their gaming experiences. Thirty-three of the participants were male and between the ages of sixteen and thirty-seven, with an average age of twenty-four. The four female participants were between the ages of sixteen and thirty-nine, with an average age of twenty-nine.

The explorative approach of the study also extended to single-player games. I decided to focus on Let's Play videos, a format that became popular several years ago on platforms like YouTube. The idea of Let's Play videos, known as LPs by their devotees, is simple: one or more people play a video game while recording the content with screen capture software and providing live, often humorous commentary. Let's Players, as they are called, upload episodes usually between 15–30 minutes long until they have completed the game. Others can then watch the playthrough and hear the commentary. More recently, Let's Players have started making live recordings of their faces during playthrough. (This is especially popular with horror games.) The 'facecam' view appears in a corner of the video.

In Germany, LP videos grew enormously popular between 2010 and 2013. Stars of the scene now have large fanbases and play full-time. The channel of the most popular German player, Gronkh, has over 4.8 million subscribers and features new videos daily. Following Gronkh is his long-time friend Sarazar, with around 1.9 million subscribers, and the gamer group PietSmiet, with around 2.3 million subscribers (all counts as of 2020). The numbers are even higher in the English-speaking world. The most popular of the international Let's Players receive many hundreds of thousands and sometimes millions of views per episode.

LP videos are a valuable source in this study because Let's Players, in their efforts to create entertaining videos, continually narrate their emotional experiences. From an ethnographic standpoint, of course, Let's Players do not necessarily articulate 'authentic' emotional experiences with playful virtual violence. Though Let's Players present themselves as normal people who enjoy gaming and want to share their fun with others, the most successful of them are professional entertainers who earn tidy sums from advertising revenue. Their emotional experiences are inextricably tied to cultural and economic practices designed to maximise the entertainment value of the videos for their viewers. Nevertheless, or perhaps precisely for that reason, LP videos are ethnographically interesting. As key figures of video game culture, Let's Players indicate which emotional experiences with playful virtual violence are possible, usual, desirable, or even taboo. They are representatives of an everyday form of gaming who post videos that shape behaviours in the gaming world. In terms of practice theory, Let's Play is a hub for the routinisation of interaction with video game violence. For this work, I analysed 310 Let's Play videos, with a total running time of around 118 hours and an average duration of 23 minutes per video. The selection of videos covered the following single-player games (sorted by the number of episodes analysed): *Grand Theft Auto V, Tomb Raider, Skyrim, Dead Space 3, Battlefield 3* and *4, Assassin's Creed 4, Outlast, Spec Ops: The Line, Max Payne 3, Hitman, Slender,* and *Crysis 2.* After gathering sufficient observations for particular emotional experiences in one type of game, I moved to others in search of different emotional experiences.

I collected additional context from analysing viewer comments for LP videos on YouTube, which can number into the thousands per episode. I used qualitative data analysis software (MAXQDA) to comb through a total of 145,000 comments for keywords and times (pegged to pivotal moments in the playthrough) and then evaluated them qualitatively. The point was not to analyse the pleasure of viewers while watching the videos. Rather, I understood their comments as a form of emotional communication that relates to the gaming and communicative practices of Let's Players so as to learn more about the emotions of players in general.

To better understand how the emotional experiences with playful virtual violence have evolved, I analysed 500 game reviews and 100 other articles from video game magazines between the years 1983 and 2014. The first German video game magazine, *TeleMatch*, appeared in 1982/83, around the same time that the popular arcade games of the1970s came to living rooms in the form of home game consoles. Methodologically, I followed the working principles of historical ethnography (Wietschorke, 2014) and the history of emotions (Plamper 2013) as I examined past emotional experiences to sharpen my analysis of those in the present (Scheer 2011, 74). I sifted through the articles for descriptions of emotional experiences with video games in texts, pictures, and other visual materials. This was less frequent than one might suppose, since most video game reviews were restricted to discussions of technical developments and fairly neutral accounts of gameplay, though some authors provided lively reports of their personal experiences.

Besides *TeleMatch*, the other dominant German video game magazines of the 1980s that I consulted were *Happy Computer Spielesonderteil* and *Power Play*. Starting in the early 1990s, more and more gaming publications appeared, some geared especially to PC or console games, resulting in a great variety of outlets. My 1990s sources consist of magazines as different as *Amiga Games, Amiga Joker, ASM, Mega Fun, PC Joker, PC Player, Play Time, Power Play,* and *Video Games.* With the new millennium, print magazines for gamers began their slow but inevitable decline. Accordingly, most of the articles I consider after 2000 were published online, chiefly in *Gamestar* and *PC Games.*

The data was evaluated qualitatively with the help of the software program MAXQDA based on the principles of grounded theory (GT) (Strauss & Corbin, 1998) and tailored to the particularities of ethnographic research and the analysis of emotional practices (Breidenstein et al. 2015, 124–38; Emerson, Fretz, & Shaw 2011, 171–200). The computer-assisted coding of emotional practices is particularly challenging because any emotional practice can only be understood based on an intimate knowledge of its sociocultural surroundings. For instance, when a player calls another player a 'noob' (i.e., a beginner), the intention could either be to insult or to tease affectionately. Coding such phrases as particular kinds of emotional practices (e.g., as a practice of insulting or a practice of teasing and friendship) involves careful ethnographic interpretation.

While the first phase of coding – explorative and inductive – resulted in a large collection of data reflecting the variety and heterogeneity of emotional practices with playful virtual violence, a second phase was needed to carve out key facets by comparing and aggregating the interpretations, differentiating and reassigning earlier strands, and developing clear criteria for attributions. Strauss and Corbin call this *axial* coding 'because coding occurs around the axis of a category, linking categories at the level of properties and dimensions' (Strauss & Corbin 1998, 123). The central task here was to determine which emotional practices and emotional experiences show 'repeated patterns' (p. 130) and then to cluster them into categories for more granular comparison. Finally, I worked to achieve empirical saturation by applying selective coding (p. 143–61), which is to say that I focussed on the dominant kinds of emotional practices in my field. Unlike typical GT studies, my work does not aim at creating an empirically grounded *theory,* but instead aims at the thick description of emotional experiences. The following Sections describe emotional experiences that are enacted through playful virtual violence.

3 Feeling through Virtual Bodies

It is 1983. The young video game journalist Helge Andersen has a problem. 'Shoot 'em up' games, in which players steer their spacecraft or other devices to shoot at pixelated figures from a top-down or side-view perspective, are all the rage. He finds them silly, but they nevertheless exercise a certain fascination over him. In an article for the German video game magazine *TeleMatch* he describes the experience of playing a new game:

> And here we go! Bang! Flash! A crackling erupts as I score a direct hit. It feels like the joystick is going to break off. All the while, I say to myself: shoot 'em ups are dumb! But they can't be that dumb, because I can't stop playing some of these games. . . . Whoom, that one hit! . . . And now it's time to proceed, concentrated, with a system. . . . Now or never: left, right, button, button, shield . . . ! What a blast![3]

Andersen's fun emerges from what I call the audiovisual 'wow effect', which is experienced nowhere more powerfully than when blowing things up. Andersen is one of the first in the German-speaking world to describe the pleasure of video game violence, but he is by no means the last. The articulation of the wow effect is an emotional practice in which video game journalists of the 1980s and 1990s frequently engaged.

In the 1990s, games moved from 2D environments to more sophisticated 3D worlds, in which violence became more graphic. One of the first action games fully playable from the first-person perspective was the 1992 *Ultima Underworld: The Stygian Abyss*. Video game journalists celebrated the realism of its combat: 'The mouse allows you to swing your weapon about and finely mete out your blows, while the bloody effects can be seen up close'.[4] In 1994, one reviewer described the space battles in the *Star Wars* game *Rebel Assault*: 'A pair of TIE fighters screech by my ship on the right with a deafening thunder, while on the left, an Imperial fighter burns up in a giant explosion under the hiss of my laser cannons'.[5] A review of the first-person shooter *Doom 2: Hell on Earth* contains a screenshot of a scene where a player's chain gun perforates a zombie with bullets (recommended example). The caption underneath reads: 'A more beautiful way to die: zombies stand no chance against a chain gun'.[6]

---

[3] Andersen, H. (1983). Schnell, schneller, superschnell. *Telematch*, March 1983(4–5), 18–19. www .kultpower.de/archiv/heft_telematch_1983-03_seite18

[4] Magenauer, M. (1992). Ultima Underworld: The Stygian Abyss. *PC Joker*, 1992(2), 50. www .kultboy.com/index.php?site=t&id=11367&s=1

[5] Hengst, M. (1994). Rebel Assault. *Power Play*, 1994(1), 46–7, p. 46. www.kultboy.com/index .php?site=t&id=3346

[6] Hengst, M. (1994). Hell on Earth: Die Zahl des Tiers. *Power Play*, 1994(11), 38–40, p. 38. www .kultboy.com/index.php?site=t&id=514

What is operative here is 'more beautiful'. For the pleasure experienced in video game violence, it matters whether an enemy spaceship disappears quietly or erupts in a loud animated explosion; whether a zombie simply falls over or is thrown to the ground in a hail of bullets. The journalist Heinrich Lenhardt summed it up in a 1994 review of the fantasy action game *The Elder Scrolls: Arena*: 'The satisfaction of cutting up hideous orcs is especially high thanks to the striking graphics and exciting sound effects'.[7]

These excerpts show that the enjoyment of audiovisual effects of digital violence has been a central facet in the pleasure derived from video games since they first appeared on the market. A look at Let's Play videos shows that this remains true today. In an episode featuring the 2013 *Grand Theft Auto V*, the Let's Player Gronkh takes on a band of Chinese gangsters. Cars fly into the air and a huge fuel tank explodes after being hit by machine gun fire. The action is narrated by Gronkh's friend Sarazar, who sits beside him. 'Yeaaah, excellent!' 'Woah, very nice!' 'That's the way I like it!' 'An explosion is always good!' Sarazar's many interjections, all products of the wow effect, demonstrate the key role of virtual violence in this kind of emotional experience.

'Bam!'

Wow effects arise not only from the passive observation of destruction but also from active participation in it. Indeed, a specific vocabulary has emerged in video game culture to express just this kind of experience with playful virtual violence: 'Boom!', 'Pam!', 'Bang!', 'Pow!', 'Zap!' and, most of all, 'Bam!' These expressions are emotional practices that articulate the joy of experiencing one's effectiveness in killing an opponent, a 'bam effect'. In an episode for the game *Skyrim*, a Let's Player known as Piet happens on a pack of bandits and charges into battle (recommended example).[8] His knight, brandishing an intimidating broadsword, fells the first bandit in a single blow. 'Bam!' Piet cries, and proceeds to make short order of the others. The Let's Player Sarazar displays similar enthusiasm while playing the first-person shooter *Battlefield 3* (recommended example).[9] Sarazar, playing a marine sergeant, takes control of a heavy machine gun mounted on a Humvee and unleashes a barrage of bullets on

---

[7] Lenhardt, H. (1994). The Elder Scrolls: Arena. *PC Player*, 1994(4), 42–3, p. 43. www.kultboy.com/index.php?site=t&id=5931

[8] PietSmiet (31 July 2013). SKYRIM # 6 – Überfordert «» Let's Play The Elder Scrolls V: Skyrim | HD. Online video clip. 11:02–11:25. www.youtube.com/embed/_qNV9Dk2BMk?start=662&end=685

[9] Sarazar (29 October 2011). Let's Play Battlefield 3 #004 [German] [Full-HD] – Eine himmlische Erfahrung. Online video clip. 4:00–4:40. www.youtube.com/embed/PhVqWTs24rk?start=240&end=280

enemy operatives. As the large calibre ammo rains down on them, Sazarar exclaims, 'Baaaaam! Bam bam bam bam!'

Some 25 per cent of the Let's Play fight sequences for *Skyrim* that I examined contained at least one 'Bam!' or a variation thereof; in *Battlefield 3* and *4*, it was 40 per cent; and in the action adventure games *Tomb Raider* and *Assassin's Creed 4*, the total reached 60 per cent. Such counts indicate the high frequency with which players take pleasure in the 'bam effect'. Not coincidentally, 'Bam!' and its synonyms are onomatopoetic inventions imitating the sound of a blow – be it a fist, a sword, a bullet, or a missile. The exclamations always accompany these moments of impact, emphasising both their force and the pleasure of the player as he or she experiences the rush of vanquishing an opponent.

In digital societies, technology allows people to extend their bodies in pursuit of intense emotional experiences. The philosopher Don Ihde, whose works explore how human lives are entangled with technology, developed a model that is helpful for understanding the phenomenon. His books *Technics and Praxis* (1979) and *Technology of the Lifeworld* (1990) draw on ideas from Edmund Husserl, Martin Heidegger, and Maurice Merleau-Ponty to argue that technology is more than an artefact or tool; it is a medium shaping how human beings perceive and act in an environment. Ihde draws on a passage in *Being and Time* (first published in German in 1927) in which Heidegger observes that when beholding a hammer in action the physical object fades into the background and one's attention turns to its activity – the nail it strikes and the wood into which it drives the nail (Heidegger 2001, 98). Heidegger calls this the hammer's 'readiness-to-hand' (p. 98), the state of a technology that has gone from being an artefact to being an intrinsic part of human action and perception. Ihde finds a similar idea in Merleau-Ponty's (2002, 165–6) reading of a blind man whose cane is at once sensory organ and embodied extension. Ihde calls this kind of relationship between humans and technology 'embodiment relations, because in this use context I take the technologies into my experiencing in a particular way by way of perceiving through such technologies and through the reflexive transformation of my perceptual and body sense' (Ihde 1990, 72; see also 1979, 6–11).

The philosopher Philipp Brey (2000) notes that Ihde concentrates on the technologies of perception and does not address other technologies – cars and hammers, say. For Brey, however, technologies are extensions not only of human perception but also of motor skills (2000, 8), shaping how we navigate in and interact with the environment. In embodiment relations, technology is a medium of perception that changes the relationship of human activity to its surroundings. By extending human beings' perceptual and motor skills, technology creates new possibilities for emotional experience. Playing video games is a prime example of a popular pleasure that derives from embodiment relations with technology. Indeed, the relations they form are particularly complex, especially in the case of 3D action games. Here, technology is not simply a means to enhance perception and action within the physical environment; it simulates a virtual body through which players link their perception and action to a virtual environment.

Among gamers, the common term for virtual body is avatar – a Sanskrit word meaning 'manifestation of a divinity' (Juul & Klevjer, 2016). My understanding of avatars as *virtual* bodies follows the concept of virtuality I describe in Section 1. The avatar body is virtual not only because it is computer-mediated but also because it crucially depends on its similarity to physical bodies. Virtual bodies can only become meaningful and effective through players treating them as representations of actual bodies and using them accordingly – moving, running, jumping, crouching, exploring, killing. The function of virtual bodies in video games, in other words, emerges from the gaming experience itself. The avatar's body is constituted by the act of playing a video game and the medium through which players experience it. In the words of the video game theorist Rune Klevjer (2006, 10): 'The avatar is the embodied manifestation of the player's engagement with the "gameworld"; it is the player incarnated'. Crucially, the avatar does not mediate between the human body and the *actual* physical environment – as is the case with eyeglasses, say. Rather, it relates the human body to a *virtual* environment. The embodiment relation between player and avatar ensures that the movements on the screen can be perceived and performed as actions of virtual bodies.

It is only in light of the embodiment relation between player and avatar that the significance of the 'bam effect' becomes apparent. Unlike the 'wow effect', which can occur while watching a movie as well as when playing a video game, the 'bam effect' signals the pleasure of a deeply embodied emotional experience.

Domination

The pleasure in the 'bam effect' has a social dimension as well. In a Let's Play video of the 2013 *Tomb Raider*, Sarazar, in the persona of Lara Croft, faces a masked enemy bearing a large bulletproof shield (recommended example).[10] After a series of evasive manoeuvres, Sarazar stabs him with an arrow. 'That's all you got, asshole?' he asks. As the opponent mounts a new attack, Sarazar

---

[10] Sarazar (8 April 2013). Let's Play Tomb Raider #038 – Das Ende einer Monarchie [FINALE] [Full-HD] [German]. Online video clip. 0:45–1:20. www.youtube.com/embed/k4Zz99UADUU?start=45&end=80

continues to bait him. 'Come on, let's dance!' 'I can do the waltz!' Sarazar adroitly dodges a machete swipe and counters with a blow to the leg. The enemy falls to his knees and Sarazar goes in for the kill. The perspective moves to a close-up shot: Lara places a shotgun under the enemy's chin and pulls the trigger. As the blood splatters, Sarazar lets out a 'Bam!' and laughs. 'Now that's an execution kill', he adds, his voice dropping deeper.

Though only 35 seconds long, the clip contains several forms of emotional experience. First is the pleasure in Sarazar's 'Bam!' as he pummels his opponent. Second is the fearlessness he demonstrates by hurling insults ('That's all you got, asshole?'; 'Come on, let's dance!'). Third is the superiority signalled by his mocking laughter. As with many other Let's Players, Sarazar engages in performative forms of communication that treat computer-controlled enemies as social agents. The German sociologists Heinrich Popitz (1992) and Wolfgang Sofsky (2005) have argued that violence demonstrates superiority and, by extension, power. In video games, players make playful allusions to the social implications of violence as they enact feelings of social superiority by dominating others through their virtual bodies.

The pleasure in dominating others is particularly pronounced in online multiplayer games, where players implicitly understand that there is a human being behind every enemy avatar. Gronkh, the best-known Let's Player in Germany, describes the difference to single player games during a session of *GTA Online*: 'It's pretty awesome, playing against other players, I gotta say. That gives you a totally different kick'.[11] The significance of the difference is something that many of the gamers I interviewed stressed. Petator, a 32-year-old male player, observed:

> What's so exciting about [multiplayer shooters] is that there's somebody, who knows how many kilometres away from me, just like me, sitting in front of the computer with a headset on and is annoyed that he was slower than me. That's totally fun in online games. It was already fun for me ten years ago with *Counter-Strike*, because I knew: 'Ha ha, now you're miffed, ha ha!'

The pleasure taken in frustrating others intensifies when opponents lose points or valuable items. In the multiplayer zombie survival game *DayZ*, the death of an avatar is permanent, and the player must start again at the beginning. This creates opportunity for a cruel form of domination. Sixteen-year-old Joey described how he likes to find a hidden spot and from there pick off players with his rifle. 'You aim at them and you know that they will die soon. Only they don't know it. That is so cool, this feeling, because you know that they have

---

spent four days [collecting equipment]. And now they're going to die'. It was clear that Joey enjoys contemplating the anger and frustration of the opponent ahead of time. Bernd, a 22-year-old gamer, told me what it feels like to kill an opponent and take his possessions:

> It's this sense that he's feeling like shit, and you've just shown him that you are better. And if you then notice that he starts flaming [insulting the attacker and getting angry in the in-game chat] then you're even more happy about it! That feeling is really awesome, definitely.

Though I couldn't see him, I detected a sly smile on Bernd's face. It should become clear, the domination of an opponent is a powerful factor in the pleasure of virtual violence. Yet for the people I interviewed, the act of domination is not altogether serious. It contains an element of playfulness and is part of the thrill of feeling superior to others.

When video game culture first formed, most players were male, and that remains true today, at least for mainstream action games; in other game genres, the picture has changed significantly.[12] The experiences of domination I came across in my research mostly involved male players, which raises the question whether pleasure in video game violence is connected to specific ideas of masculinity. For ethnographers, it is less productive to ask *why* so many male players find video game violence fun than to explore whether ideas of masculinity amplify the pleasure from video game violence.

Although the field of game studies has no shortage of literature on gender theory, few studies have addressed the relationship between masculinity and taking pleasure in video game violence. (For a notable exception, see Jansz, 2005.) Of course, many males in player groups engage in posturing displays and occasionally drop homophobic jokes and misogynistic comments (Nardi 2010, 152–7). Judging by the emotional practices of the players, however, concrete links between video game violence and specific notions of masculinity are rare. An exception can be found in emotional practices that express pleasure in video game violence through male-connoted sexual acts. Words like 'fuck' or 'bang' are regularly used by male players as synonyms for video game violence. It can occur in the annunciation of violence, as when the Let's Player Hardi, waiting to ambush an enemy in the stealth action game *Hitman: Absolution*, says, 'Oh, I'm going to fuck you right in the ass, boy'.[13] Other times it serves to emphasise

---

[12] For Germany, see a 2014 study on media use by teenagers, which included specific questions about the use of violent video games. www.mpfs.de/fileadmin/files/Studien/JIM/2014/JIM_Studie_2014.pdf

[13] PietSmiet (28 November 2012). Let's Play Hitman Absolution #009 [German] [HD] – Eiskalt hingerichtet. Online video clip. 9:45–10:10. www.youtube.com/embed/QicbJSjJ3Ak?start=585&end=610

violence after the fact, such as when a player of *Counter-Strike* comments on a kill with the words: 'I fucked you, you noob'. The frequency of sexual comments like these varies strongly. The Let's Player Sarazar, and many of those I played with during my research, do not use them, whereas other players use them regularly. Less common than the inclusion of terms such as 'fuck', but just as significant, if not more so, is the use of the English word 'rape'. It is rarely heard in German-language Let's Play videos, but occurs routinely in the text and voice chat channels for shooters and other multiplayer games. During a heated discussion after a gruelling fight in *DayZ*, the user Petator's opines, 'You can actually only punish people with one thing: you simply have to rape them'.

To better understand what players mean when they use these sexualised terms, we need to listen to the players themselves. Here is Petator, who did not mince words:

> So, to fuck someone, yes, that's a sexual act, where you are definitely the active one, and there is a passive one. And when you say, 'I'm fucking somebody', then you're definitely the active one, and somebody who's actively fucking somebody else is definitely also the dominant one, because he's the more active one. Do you understand what I mean?

Asked about the meaning of 'rape', he replied:

> Destroy them! Just stomp them into the ground. Shoot them down, don't give them any chances, total overkill, that's what it means. Wear them down in a game so much that they're sick and tired. Rage quit! Rage quit on the other team! That's pretty much what it is.

A 'rage quit' – another instance of English used by German players – is when a player abruptly leaves a game out of anger. The term is paradigmatic for the other side of domination in multiplayer games: the experience of one's own inferiority. It is what makes defeat a 'rape' in the first place. For it is only because players become angry and frustrated after losing that they can be humiliated. Petator was quite frank about that:

> Yeah, it's definitely about humiliation as well. Also with a rape, it's also about humiliation, I think. I, I don't know, I've never looked into the psychological aspects of a rape. But I could imagine that's part of it. If somebody rapes somebody else, you have total control over them, you have them in your hand, you know? And you do this with the sickest possible violence. And that's what we do with others online. We dominate them, as it were. We take everything from them that we can take online [laughs sheepishly].

The use of highly sexualised language by Petator and many of the others I interviewed underscores the experience of domination in video game violence.

The question that needs to be asked is whether the targeted use of sexualised language expresses a further dimension of pleasure that emerges from the confluence of video game violence, domination, and masculinity.

In answering that question, I take the view of Candace West and Don H. Zimmerman that masculinity, and sexuality in general, are products of social, cultural, and emotional processes. 'A person's gender', they write, 'is not simply an aspect of what one is, but, more fundamentally, it is something that one does, and does recurrently, in interaction with others' (1987, 140). Specific ways of feeling play a crucial role in what West and Zimmerman call 'doing gender'. Expressions of emotion can be a form of doing gender and vice versa. Stephanie A. Shields et al. (2006) write, 'Shared beliefs about emotion assist in defining and maintaining beliefs about gender and gender-as-difference. . . . Beliefs about emotion reveal the distinctive 'how' of being a gendered person: Doing emotion . . . signals one's genuineness as female or male, feminine or masculine' (p. 67). The particular ways of doing emotion that count as feminine or masculine depend on social, cultural, and historical factors (Borutta & Verheyen, 2010). Context is crucial: think of male fans at football matches who cry openly when their club loses but who would be ashamed to do so in public anywhere else. Emotional practices with male gender connotations exist for a wide variety of individuals and sociocultural situations.

The use of terms such as 'fuck' and 'rape' to articulate experiences of domination mobilises a particularly clichéd form of male emotion: the enjoyment taken in the aggressive sexual penetration of other individuals. Such sexually charged emotives can serve as articulations of a certain type of masculinity within a social group. This does not mean that all players take this masculinity or its male-connoted feelings seriously. Nor does it mean that the pleasure they experience is based on a physical affirmation of certain male stereotypes. To be certain, emotional practices provide real validation for some players. More typically, however, players *interact playfully* with this stereotypical, sexualised idea of masculinity in pursuit of enjoyable emotional experiences.

Affected Bodies

So far, I have focused on the emotional experiences associated with perpetrating video game violence. But equally important for understanding pleasure in video game violence is how it is experienced by its 'victims', which all action gamers are at some point or another. The experience of violence perpetrated on one's virtual body can induce feelings of stress, menace, fear, and sometimes even physical pain. Yet these feelings are also part of the gaming experience and, for many, part of what makes it enjoyable.

The cover of the very first issue of *TeleMatch* (recommended example) offers an allegory for a playful response to threats in video games.[14] It depicts Pac-Man as a round yellow head with hands and feet – a highly abstracted representation of the human body – as he runs from several ghosts, who will take a life if they touch him. His face epitomises pleasure in the face of peril: he shoots a hurried glance at his pursuers but seems to be having fun, his face a big toothy grin. The unique mixture of stress and fun is echoed in the earliest reviews of action games. In the issue of *TeleMatch* with the Pac-Man cover, a journalist describes the 'superfast attack game' *Nautilus*:

> There's not much time left: as commander of the Nautilus, an attack submarine fully equipped with an arsenal of thunderbolt torpedoes, you have to make insanely fast decisions and act quickly. The threats are unending, as a heavily-armed destroyer on the ocean's surface has taken up the hunt for the Nautilus, with depth charges and rockets that react to each movement. . . . Despite the barrage of attacks, your torpedoes find their target. Yet will the Nautilus survive? Will your nerves hold out? Who, in the end, will win the fight?[15]

The idea that threat is nerve-wracking yet thrilling is also frequently expressed in the communicative practices of Let's Play videos. Moments of peril are accompanied by cursing ('Shit!', 'Fuck!', 'What the fuck!'), word repetitions ('Dude, dude, dude!', 'Man, man, man!'), exclamations ('Fuck me!' and 'Oh, boy!'), and interjections ('Owwwwww!', 'Woah!', 'Oh!', 'Ay ay ay!', and 'Ahhhhh!'). The expressions are the same that people outside the gaming world use when experiencing a threatening situation or when empathising with the threatening situations of others. In action games, they are particularly prevalent. A total of 65 per cent of the single-player Let's Play fight sequences I examined and 85 per cent of the cases when players' avatars are subjected to violence and can't fight back contained one or more of these expressions. These facets of experience make up a considerable portion of the pleasure in video game violence.

Being the victim of virtual violence often elicits responses in the player's physical body. 'Everybody who has experienced an exciting video game', a reviewer of a space shooter writes in 1984, 'knows that feeling when you feel the action so close to your skin that it takes your breath away and your pulse quickens'.[16] Other reviewers speak of games whose 'realistic animation . . .

---

[14] *Telematch* 1983(1). www.kultpower.de/archiv/heft_telematch_1983-01_seite1
[15] Nautilus: Ein superschnelles Angriffsspiel für Atari-Computer. *Telematch*, 1983(1), 48. www .kultpower.de/archiv/heft_telematch_1983-01_seite48
[16] Forman, T. (1984). Sinistar, der Schrecken des Universums, kommt! *Telematch*, 1984, H. 3, S. 66–8, hier: S. 66. www.kultpower.de/archiv/heft_telematch_1984-03_seite66

makes players wince at each incoming shot'[17] or whose 'nerve-racking action' makes 'the blood boil'.[18] Pearls of sweat, cramped fingers, racing hearts, and 'adrenaline kicks' all feature as central elements in journalists' descriptions of video game experience. The same thing is true for *Let's Play* videos: Gronkh has to 'sweat piss'[19] during an action scene; for Sarazar, a battle is 'still in the bones'[20]; Brammen gets 'hard nipples' after an explosion[21]; and Hardi, writing about a scary sound in *Dead Space 3*, states, 'No joke, just now everything inside me tightened up. Just like this [he makes a face for the facecam]: mmmmyeah! God, what a sound, man'.[22]

This does not mean that being on the receiving end of virtual violence is stronger or deeper than being on the giving end. Moreover, some of the experiences described by video game journalists and players (such as breaking out in a sweat) correspond to actual bodily processes, while others (describing a moment as 'toe-curling', say) function as metaphors for an intense physical response. In both cases, however, the virtual violence players receive is experienced at a somatic level. Of course, players' bodies are never subjected to actual physical violence. And they always have the option of removing themselves from a threating situation, either by distancing themselves mentally ('It's just a game') or by quitting. The players who decide to stick around willingly submit their physical bodies to the excitations of seeing their avatars under constant threat.

Nowhere is that more true than in horror games. A particularly good example is *Slender: The Eight Pages*. The game begins in the first-person perspective in the middle of a dark forest. The player has no weapons, only a flashlight, and its batteries last only for a short while. As the player moves through the woods, menacing sound effects play in the background. The goal is to collect eight handwritten notes warning of a tall, pale faceless entity known as Slender Man.

---

[17] Encounter. *Happy Computer Spielesonderheft*, 1985(1), 44. www.kultpower.de/archiv/heft_hap pycomputer_spielesonderheft-1_seite44

[18] Gaksch, M., & Lenhardt, H. (1988). Gradius (Nemesis). *Power Play*, 1988(4), 88. www .kultpower.de/archiv/heft_powerplay_1988-04_seite88

[19] Gronkh (22 December 2013). GTA V (GTA 5) [HD+] #098 – KRIEG gegen das FIB!! Let's Play GTA 5 (GTA V). Online video clip. 6:40–6:50. www.youtube.com/embed/z9xeXCeNqQM? start=400&end=410

[20] Sarazar (6 April 2013). Let's Play Tomb Raider #036 – Kampf gegen die Untoten [Full-HD] [German]. Online video clip. 8:25–8:35. www.youtube.com/embed/iOer2ZNjXfM? start=505&end=515

[21] PietSmiet (29 October 2013). BATTLEFIELD 4 SINGLEPLAYER # 1 – Die Saga beginnt «» Let's Play Battlefield 4/BF4 | HD. Online video clip. 23:30–23:40. www.youtube.com/embed/ L8HKGZM_YnY?start=1410&end=1420

[22] PietSmiet (11 February 2013). Let's Play Dead Space 3 #005 [German] [HD] – Auf Shuttlesuche. Online video clip. 5:00–5:35. www.youtube.com/embed/LWqnmTqYU4Q? start=300&end=335

All the while, said Slender Man lurks in the darkness and can appear at any time. If he comes into contact with a player, or if a player looks at him too long, the game is over.

Slender has become very popular on Let's Play channels in large part due to the use of the facecam perspective, allowing viewers to see the real-time physical responses of players as they cope with fear and stress and laugh at their own reactions. The first three Let's Play videos for *Slender* on the *Gamestar* YouTube channel have received between 500,000 and 1.5 million views each. Let's Players Martin and Daniel have little prior knowledge of the gameplay as they start.[23] In the top left corner, the facecam shows their faces under sparse lighting. They find the first page and an eerie pulsating sound can be heard. Both cry, 'Uahhh!' and Martin – who is only there to watch – reflexively pulls his face back from the screen. 'I hate this kind of music'. Shortly after, the Slender Man teleports suddenly into view accompanied by a loud bass tone, and the two of them scream, 'Woaaaah!' 'There he is! There he is!' Daniel yells, as he commands his character to run away. Martin see-saws back and forth in front of the screen. Smiles follow their screams.

The two play the game over several episodes. In one scene, they arrive at a dark tunnel (recommended example).[24] 'Don't go in there! Don't go in there!' a panicked Martin yells. Yet go in they must, because one of the eight pages is glued to a wall inside. Daniel quickly grabs the page and a dreadful din rings out. 'Uaaahhhh!' both yell, and Daniel flees further into the tunnel. Martin is frightened. 'You can't go through this tunnel!' He tells Daniel that he should at least go faster. They manage to exit the tunnel on the side and come across creepy ruins. Martin gathers all his courage. 'We have to go in there', he says gravely. Slowly, they peek around the first corner and see a dimly lit room. Suddenly, they hear a dissonant static sound. Daniel turns the avatar around: right in front of him is Slender Man. Both scream. The screen flickers. Gameover. 'Dude!' Daniel is stunned. 'How did he do that?' Both are quiet for a second. At this point, the facecam in the YouTube video switches to full-screen mode. Both burst out laughing. Daniel sighs. 'Woah, man!' The tension disappears from their faces and changes to relief. They decide that Martin should now play a round.

---

[23] GameTube (19 July 2012). Horror – Slender Gameplay mit Facecam #1 – Let's Play Slenderman Game German. Online video clip. 0:00–4:30. www.youtube.com/embed/W7eWF5fdrWA?start=0&end=270

[24] GameTube ((20 July 2012). Horror – Slender Gameplay mit Facecam #2 – Let's Play Slenderman Game German. Online video clip. 0:00–6:20. www.youtube.com/embed/Dali8w1-QFw?start=375&end=567

As the clip shows, the pleasure in being at the receiving end of video game violence arises from a conscious decision to expose oneself to a perceived risk. It is difficult to say *why* the body is so strongly affected by games like these. Perhaps it is part biological, such as fear of the dark, and part cultural, such as emotional routines learned from playing similar games and watching horror films. For my work, however, it is not so much *why* players feel this way as *how* they handle their physical reactions. For though the violence of video games carries no actual risk, the players physically respond as if it were real. And by putting their virtual bodies at risk, they experience their physical bodies in a new and exciting way.

Respawn

The embodiment relation that makes the risk of video game violence feel real raises another question: what happens when players' characters are injured or killed? In *Slender*, death is abstract; in others, especially those involving combat, it is appreciably more concrete. Of course, players never feel like they are actually dying, regardless of the form in which death comes. But of all the ways a player can lose a game, virtual death is not another neutral experience among others (Klastrup 2008).

Early action games of the 1970s and 80s featured abstract avatars that died after a single hit. One reason was that the manufacturers of coin-operated arcade machines wanted to maximise the amount of money they could extract from players (Tocci 2008, 192). But as video game consoles spread in the 1980s, avatars came to have many lives, giving players the possibility of replaying challenging segments multiple times before restarting. Games in the 1990s went a step further by allowing players to save their progress after dying and start there later. The re-appearance of a video game character after having been killed is known as 'respawning'. For the player Limaneel, it is a key factor in the experience of virtual death:

> Dying for me means: failed the current attempt, try again, new round, better luck next time. ... You're out for that round. Or, you have to go back to respawn. For me, it's not an actual death but an incapacitation. ... In real life, it might be something like a knockout punch, but I wouldn't see it as anything more.

By comparing virtual death to a knockout, Limaneel seems to say not only that virtual death is temporary but also that it is somehow akin to a physical process. Some recent first-person action games such as *Skyrim* or *Counter-Strike: Global Offensive* have put the corporeality of virtual death into stark relief by abruptly switching to a third-person perspective during death. The external view of the body allows players to behold the full impact of the fatal blow. A number of third-person action games, where players already see the deaths of their character from an external viewpoint, up the ante by showing the fatality in slow motion and explicit detail. Virtual death may be only temporary, but many games depict it in the most violent way possible. The player Wooshy offered an interpretation of these violent representations of death:

> The only thing humans know absolutely is that they will die. Without [this knowledge, video games] would be unable to build this element of tension . . . I think that . . . killing somebody or being killed oneself serves to create a cut in the game . . . or in one's thinking, which says something like, it's over now, this is absolute, there's nothing more.

Players respond to this 'cut' in very different ways. Some face it with detachment, as if bored; others shout 'LOL!' in surprise. Most display annoyance, disappointment, frustration, or anger. Common locutions include 'Noooooo', 'Shit!', 'Go fuck yourself!', and 'Kiss my ass!' Sometimes their words are accompanied by a physical outburst such as striking a desk or throwing the mouse. Many seek an explanation for their character's death. Some blame external circumstances: the controller failed, the avatar did not do what it was supposed to do, team members fell short, the game generated too many enemies. Others blame themselves. Most are already thinking about starting again as they watch their character die. They gather fresh courage, ponder aloud how they could do better, or announce that they will prevail next time.

I asked Pandrael, an experienced gamer, about how he responds when his character on the multiplayer online game *The Elder Scrolls Online* dies. 'For me', he said, 'it just means taking a short break. It doesn't get to me emotionally'. The no-less-experienced gamer Miralla admitted a very different reaction: 'It's the worst [laughs]. It's always awful when it happens, especially because I usually break something'. If her character dies a single time, she can cope. But after failing multiple times against a final boss, say, she may have to put the game down for several weeks, such is her frustration. In extreme instances, rage quits are common.

The level of frustration that the game produces stands in direct proportion to the excitement felt when defeating a final boss or making it to the next level. This is plainly visible in players of the *Dark Souls* games, which are known for their unforgiving difficulty. Florian Heider, in a review of the game for *Gamestar* titled 'Dying can look this beautiful!', writes: 'Four destroyed gamepads, two shattered monitors, and a chewed up keyboard cable. Giant rats in the editorial department? No, *Dark Souls* has finally been released for the PC! We show why some games are worth the suffering'.[25] Most encounters with enemies end in death and the loss of the bonus items the player has collected, and the boss fights at the end of each level are daunting. But the difficulty makes playing the game a special experience. 'Losing again after a ten-minute fight with a dragon may be devastating', Heider writes, 'but it is nothing compared to the euphoria that sets in when . . . we finally send the scaly brute to the eternal hunting grounds – hallelujah!'[26] 'I will remember the emotions that *Dark Souls* woke in me for years to come', he concludes. The intensity of the threat to the virtual body is critical; it shapes the intensity of the experience of exercising virtual violence. A victory has value when something is at stake, and what is at stake here is an emotional experience whose condition is the possibility of being frustrated. Negative emotional experiences are the price players pay for the chance of having exceptionally positive experiences. They risk frustration in the short term for singular intensity down the line.

4 Between Competition and Cooperation

Another component in the ability of playful virtual violence to create enjoyable experiences with virtual bodies is the competitive environment of gaming culture. The player Barry told me that participating competitively in multiplayer shooters is 'fun. You don't see the killing . . . you just want to measure up to other people, just as in football'. The idea of competition is closely related to concepts of contest and struggle (Tauschek 2013). For my work, competitive gaming is interesting for the comparison and hierarchy it enables – in how actors measure themselves against each other. How do competition and comparison become entangled with emotional practices, and how do the entanglements shape the enacting of pleasurable emotional experiences? Though many scholars examine competitive processes in video games, they define the key concepts differently and rarely explore the relationship between virtual violence and competition. In this Section, I consider how competitive practices contribute to emotional experiences with playful virtual violence.

Many video games employ a standard measure of success: points. Since the origin of video games, points have been a central feature because they allow players to compare their performance with past efforts and those of other players. Early gaming magazines depict point comparisons as one of the main motivations for playing video games and the basis for a particularly satisfying

---

[25]　Heider, F. (8 September 2012): So schön kann sterben sein! Dark Souls: Prepare to Die Edition im Test. *Gamestar.de*. www.gamestar.de/spiele/dark-souls-prepare-to-die-edition/test/dark_soul s_prepare_to_die_edition,48018,3004764.html

[26]　Ibid.

sense of achievement. As the editors of *TeleMatch* put it in their first edition: 'Let's indulge in the fun of being better than all the others!'[27]

Back then, 'being better than all the others' did not always mean competing against players directly. In many of the early video games, players eagerly vied with each other to be the best against the computer. Top players at arcades would enter their names or initials in high score lists for local bragging rights. Owners of game consoles and computers also compared high scores with friends. At least that is the assumption of the fictive video game expert 'Dr. Bobo' (the game journalist Boris Schneider), who spoofed video game culture in a tongue-in-cheek column for *Happy Computer*. 'An hypothesis of difficulty for any action game: If it looks easy, it's hard. If it looks hard, it's impossible. It if looks impossible, your neighbour managed it days ago'.[28] As Dr. Bobo's remark shows, the significance of points was closely connected to the perception of a game's difficulty. Many of the early reviews describe the pleasure of the challenge. As one review of the shooter *Phoenix* puts it: 'Masters shine with their astronomical scores'.[29] Only those who invest the time can develop the concentration, reaction speed, and strategic skills to become 'masters' within the gaming community.

From the beginning, the gaming world organised competitions pitting the best players against each other. *TeleMatch*'s first tournament was held in Munich in 1983 and featured the shooters *River Raid* and *Sea Quest*.[30] In these and other early games, performance was based on the number of kills, making virtual violence a central criterion for comparing video game success.

Flash forward to the present. The relationship between virtual violence and video game performance remains enshrined in video game culture, though the practices for comparison have become more diverse. For example, the most popular gaming mode in the *Battlefield* series, an online multiplayer first-person shooter, awards points for capturing enemy flags, for teamwork (helping allies, repairing vehicles), and for kills. Players can see their current scores by tapping a key, and many constantly check their 'stats'. Those with the most kills usually have the top scores, because kills provide most of points. More important, many value their overall score less than their 'kill/death ratio' (included in the scoreboard). 'You want ... 'positive stats", Petator told me. By 'positive

---

[27] TeleMatch. Das Spiel beginnt. *TeleMatch*, 1983(1), 3. www.kultpower.de/archiv/heft_tele match_1983-01_seite2

[28] Schneider, B. (1985). Aus dem Labor von Dr. Bobo. *Happy Computer Spielesonderheft*, 1, 72. www.kultpower.de/archiv/heft_happycomputer_spielesonderheft-1_seite72

[29] Die Atari-Offensive. *TeleMatch*, 1983(2–3), 32–3, p. 33. www.kultpower.de/archiv/heft_tele match_1983-02_seite32

[30] TeleMatch-Meisterschaft: Duell der Besten. *Telematch*, 1984(1), 12. www.kultpower.de/archiv/ heft_telematch_1984-01_seite12

stats', Petator means having more kills than deaths. Among frequent *Battlefield* players, those with an especially high kill/death ratio are often the objects of praise or envy.

Esports

A key reason for the popularity of online multiplayer games is that the competition with other players is more demanding than the fight against the computer and thus promises a stronger sense of achievement. A human player, according to Limaneel, 'acts and reacts, puts you under pressure, removes the pressure, tries to escape. The conflict is much more complex'. Sixteen-year-old Miralla said, 'In order to kill players, you need skill!' The need for 'skill' – German-speaking players typically use the English term – represents a challenge that elevates the experience of comparing one's performance with opponents.

It is no surprise, then, that a significant share of video game players participate in what is known as electronic sports, or esports. Players form teams (often referred to as 'clans'), follow rigorous training plans, organise trial matches, and enter competitions. Constant training and professionalisation has led devoted esports players to develop extraordinary abilities. 'In the same way traditional sports shape embodied action, elite video game play also inscribes itself on the body of players, refining over time the most nuanced yet complex circuit of action', writes T. L. Taylor (2012, 39), in the most ambitious ethnographic study on esports to date. Esport clans frequently participate in national or international leagues that are organised like those of conventional sports teams. Often, the players live hundreds of kilometres away from one another and meet online, where they train, plan strategies, and run competitions.

But the highlights for professional gamers are large offline tournaments known as LAN parties. The two events I attended took place over several days in large halls on the outskirts of German cities and contained hundreds of players, most of whom were men. Players wore professionally designed jerseys emblazoned with the logos of their sponsors. Like sports teams, the clans formed a 'line-up', pursued carefully planned strategies, and warmed up before important matches (less about warming up muscles than entering into an embodiment relation with the avatar). The games in the main tournaments consisted of *League of Legends*, *Battlefield 4*, and *Counter-Strike*, though countless others were running on the side. The competitions for the notorious multiplayer first-person shooter *Counter-Strike* followed predetermined rules with five players on each side. Teams played either as terrorists or counter-terrorists, swapping sides after several rounds. The terrorists had to place and explode a bomb, and the counter-terrorists had to prevent them. Another option was to kill the opposing team to win a round. The designations 'counterterrorist' and 'terrorist' were largely meaningless. Nothing indicated that players considered the actual political backdrop for the game. They accepted the counterterrorism plot as just one of many in competitive gaming.

An integral part of the *Counter-Strike* competitions at the LAN parties I attended was the performance of emotional practices in the physical space of the halls: periodic exclamations of 'Yeah!', 'Woohoo!', and 'Yes!'; players pumping their fists or clapping their hands; teammates' praising each other with words of encouragement – 'Good!', 'Nice, man!', 'Clean!', and 'Strong round!' – or with appreciative pats on the back. At the same time, the pressure of the competition and the ever-present spectre of defeat took their toll, leading to disappointment and frustration. It was common to see players shout 'Fuck, fuck, fuck!', 'Shit!', or 'Noooo!', pull their hair, pound on the table, or become hostile to team members.

What role does playful virtual violence have in competitive gaming experiences? In *Quest for Excitement: Sport and Leisure in the Civilizing Process* (1986), Norbert Elias argues that allusions to physical violence are a central part of conventional sports competitions. Elias writes that 'the setting of sport, like that of many other leisure-pursuits, is designed to move, to stir the emotions, to evoke tensions in the form of a controlled, a well-tempered excitement' (Elias & Dunning 1986, 48). Though Elias's ideas about the 'civilising process' do not exactly map on to emotional practice theory (Scheer 2011, 65), the quoted observation ties in to my arguments so far. Elias believes that the ability of sports to mobilise emotions derives from its being an imitation of an actual physical fight. 'Some forms of sport whose design most closely resembles that of a real battle between hostile groups have a particularly strong propensity for stirring up emotions, for evoking excitement' (1986, 49). The resemblance to real battles enables emotionally intense comparison:

> Sports contests enable people to gain victory over others in a physical struggle without physically hurting them. The resolution of the battle-tension and the exertion through victory can have an exhilarating and purifying effect. One can enjoy the confirmation of one's own worth without bad conscience, a justified accretion of self-love in the certainty that the struggle was fair. In that way, sport provides for self-love without bad conscience. (49; n.13, 289)

From an ethnographic perspective, the value judgment that sports activities have an 'exhilarating and purifying effect' is problematic. But the observation that physical confrontation allows a 'confirmation of one's own worth' is nevertheless useful. It is what makes confrontation a competitive process in which the victorious experience 'self-love' and pride.

Esport players take it as given that their experiences are similar to those of participants in physical sports. *Counter-Strike* competitions adopt the conventions of traditional sports and embed them in the game play. As Klaus Schönberger and Christian Ritter (2017) argue, contemporary media practices often emerge through an interplay of persistence and recombination. This is also true of esports, where emotional practices themselves are not so much novel as recombined from persisting practices in traditional sports cultures and tailored to video game play. In traditional sports such as football, competitive comparison during physical confrontations with opponents facilitates enjoyable emotional experiences. In video gaming, playful virtual violence is intertwined with similar routines and practices that are not only accepted in our society but even considered desirable.

Team Players

> Protective magic zips through the air and . . . excited chatter about the best tactic fills the team message channel. Then, the enormous stone portal opens – the clock is running. We have ten minutes to claim the altar stone. The enemy team consists of four warriors, two elementalists, and two healers. The line-up is good but not invincible. The healers are the first targets. While the lads are busy saving their own lives . . . our team can dispatch the others. Fireballs roar through the air, blades whirr, the first enemy casualties litter the ground. But then we lose a healer and watch our hit points climb. Kyra Ironblade, a warrior with a secondary profession as replacement doctor, sneaks through the hidden canyons, reaches the dead healer, and brings him back to life. Together they rush to the altar. While Kyra provides cover, the healer revives fallen team members. In the last remaining moments, they capture the altar. Victory![31]

This is Petra Schmitz, in the introduction to her review of the 2005 MMORPG *Guild Wars*, describing the thrill of her team's hard-won victory. The same kind of pleasure can be found among players of *The Elder Scrolls Online* (TESO), an MMORPG I observed as a participant. Theoretically, one can master the adventures on the continent of Tamriel in isolation, but many players prefer to join forces as they face computer-controlled monsters, whether in PvE (player versus environment) or in PvP (player versus player) mode. Like many who are looking for teammates, I met Tommy, MauMau, Aruto, and Julia on the game's chat channel. We first played together in a PvE dungeon, where four to twelve players fight through a cavern full of computer-controlled monsters. Via voice

---

[31] Schmitz, P. (12 June 2005). Guild Wars im Test. Tolles Online-Rollenspiel ohne Grundgebühr. *Gamestar.de*. www.gamestar.de/spiele/guild-wars/test/guild_wars,33439,1453979.html

chat, I learned that they knew each other in real life (Tommy and MauMau were brothers) and had played *World of Warcraft* (WoW) for quite some time. But, like me, they were beginners to *TESO*, so we all had to struggle.

We cleared the first dungeon straight away only because our avatars happened to complement each other very well. Teams playing MMORPGs commonly choose avatars with different strengths. The 'holy trinity' of basic roles in the MMORPG world consists of the 'damage dealer', 'tank', and 'healer', and this is the arrangement we decided on. The interaction of avatars with differing roles and abilities enables particular emotional experiences. Cooperation in battle – 'togetherness', as one player put it – generates its own emotional quality, because, as Schmitz writes, 'Working with many others on a large task is ... a good feeling'.[32] My *TESO* team experienced this feeling even though we were just a small group. We played regularly together over the next few weeks, exploring Tamriel, mastering various dungeons, gifting one another valuable loot, laughing about our mistakes, and watching our avatars grow stronger. The point of our efforts was 'to survive the challenge as a team, in the group', Aruto told me in a subsequent interview. We stuck together and enjoyed the fruits of our alliance. Other players in MMORPGs or in games such as *DayZ* have similar experiences. The player Pumba, talking about *DayZ*, commented, 'Just as in any other online game in which you play together with others, the feeling is great: you've accomplished something together, it worked, you set a goal, and everything worked wonderfully'.

After we had reached higher avatar levels, we decided to play in PvP mode, where up to several hundred players from three different factions fight at once, all trying to kill opponents, take their castles, and capture their flags over a vast territory with multiple arenas, some involving major battles, others minor skirmishes. One day, as Tommy, MauMau, and I were hanging out with our avatars near one of our smaller outposts, an overwhelming enemy force of ten players attacked us. At first we hid. Then we decided to spring into battle, accepting the likelihood that we'd get 'wiped out' in the process. I loaded my 'ulti', an ultimate skill that creates a magical shield around a team for several seconds. Under its protection, we charged the enemy forces head-on. Tommy, whose avatar served as our tank, bore the brunt of the damage, and held the enemies in place with magical claws; I cast magic spells that dealt damage to everyone around us; and MauMau, an archer, invoked a curse that disarmed their magic. We continued to fight until, much to our surprise, we had killed all ten combatants without suffering a single casualty. 'Hey, did that really just

---

[32] Schmitz, P. (4 March 2011). Rift Test. Riss mit Schmiss. *Gamestar.de*. www.gamestar.de/spiele/rift/test/rift,46088,2321409.html

happen?' we wondered over the voice chat. We broke out in cheers. 'Epic! Epic! Epic!' MauMau yelled, using a common English-language superlative among MMORPG players to describe exceptional experiences and memorable events. When I later asked them to name a particularly unforgettable moment, it was this episode that Tommy recalled:

> That was of course a very, very nice moment. . . . We defeated a much larger force through clever coordination of our abilities. So . . . yeah. And it's such a surprising moment, even more so when you experience that with buddies or friends. . . . I'll still be telling my grandkids about it.

We all laughed, but it was true: the battle was extraordinary, and to this day stands out among all my *TESO* experiences.

In the search of experiences like ours, *TESO* players venture into ever-more-difficult levels and against ever-larger groups. In so-called endgames, players in PvE mode must come together in groups as large as twelve to defeat the strongest bosses. (In *WoW*, as many as forty players may be needed.) These groups are mostly composed of members from larger 'guilds', which can consist of many dozens of players. The PvE guild events are called 'raids' because of the loot (weapons, armor, objects) that players can collect. Pirou, both a 'guild leader' and a 'raid leader', commands raids multiple times a week. The team must be perfectly synchronised to stand a chance of winning: the damage dealers must unleash major DPS (damage per second), the tanks have to 'hold aggro' (draw attacks), and the healers have to employ their 'ults' at the proper time. Everyone must remember their 'buff food' (usable objects that raise attribute points), and the 'skill rotation' (the arrangement of avatar abilities in the fight) needs to be just right. I participated in a raid that repeatedly tried to master a twelve-player dungeon – without success. When asked about the appeal of regular raids, the player Limaneel replied: 'Sometimes we spent weeks trying to defeat the same boss before we succeeded. It was a sense of achievement that's almost impossible to describe. You might feel something similar if you, I don't know, if you win a football tournament or something'.

The comparisons with other sports cultures I noted earlier account for the positive emotions that players feel when they master a challenge. At the same time, the players emphasised the importance of cooperation in amplifying the sense of achievement. Lela, a guild leader, explained why:

> It's definitely an experience of success, you know? It's generally . . . when you can hold out for a long time against an overpowering opponent – that is a sense of achievement. . . . And because you share this in the group, you enjoy it even more, because you've achieved something together as a team.

The group is not only a vehicle for pleasure; the experience of collective fighting has its own unique quality. The members of the group know the positive feeling of sharing their hard-won success with each other. In order to understand the dynamic, it is helpful to regard player groups as what Barbara Rosenwein calls 'emotional communities', that is, 'groups in which people adhere to the same norms of emotional expression and value – or devalue – the same or related emotions' (2006, 2). Rosenwein emphasises that emotional communities exist on multiple levels and can overlap, merge, or compete with one another: 'Imagine ... a large circle within which are smaller circles, none entirely concentric but rather distributed unevenly within the given space' (2006, 24). The idea that player groups constitute informal, ever-changing, yet persistent emotional communities is compatible with emotional practice theory. The question is the extent to which emotional practices within player groups mobilise and regulate emotions, forge emotional norms, and enact emotional experiences *between* players.

The first striking feature of emotional communities in the gaming world is the braggadocio regarding personal achievements. The voice chat channels of online games are full of examples. Here are some typical statements made by *Counter-Strike* players: 'Boom, man, did you see how I finished him?' 'Yeah, ha ha, did you see that? The mouse twitched, and right in the head!' 'I totally ruled with the auto-sniper man – bam, bam! You should have seen it'. 'I'm such an animal, man!' 'That was a brilliant headshot, right? I thought it was pretty awesome!' 'Man, right now I've got the best moves with the AWP [sniper rifle]! The whole time, 180 degrees and headshot!' While the examples in *Counter-Strike* describe single actions, *TESO* players tend to brag about entire battles. MauMau, after destroying countless enemies in PvP mode while defending a castle, remarked, 'Wow! I killed a lot of people before the castle fell! I bet I killed a hundred!' Players' unabashed expressions of joy after successfully killing opponents reveals the specific emotional conventions of gaming culture. The emotional communities of player groups serve as projection screens of emotional experiences that not only tolerate pleasure in playful virtual violence but – crucially – convey it as something desirable. Within the groups, bragging is an emotional practice that communicates one's own achievements, shares them with others, solicits recognition from other players, and works to mobilise enjoyable emotional experiences. So while bragging about experiences of mastery and domination may seem focused on individuals, it nevertheless contains an important social dimension as a form of communication and a means of facilitating group emotions.

The second emotional practice common among gamer groups is mutual praise. Shouts of 'Good!', 'Nice!', 'Clean!', and 'You animal!' echo across the voice channels; in chats, the message 'gj' (good job) is everywhere. Recognition is not reserved exclusively for the best players. Even beginners, like me, receive praise. Of course, it was not my gaming skills that earned me words of encouragement such as 'You animal!' or 'High skill PhD' but my participation in an emotional community where praise was an established routine. Players implicitly understand that they can intensify their pleasure when they communicate their group's success and frame their gaming experiences as enjoyable through boasting and praise. 'I enjoy it too when playing', the player Pandora told me. 'That's why I dole out so much praise'. When I asked if she is proud of her boyfriend, Lee, an accomplished *Counter-Strike* player, she replied, 'At the beginning [when the two first started playing together], I was always so super proud, because he just totally mowed down the opponents'.

In online multiplayer games, the experience of playful virtual violence – whether as the perpetrator or the victim – generates a sense of belonging based on practices of mutual affection, aid, protection, boasting, praise, recognition, and separating 'us' from 'them'. Playful virtual violence is, to a large extent, a *cooperative* pleasure in which gamers share and communicate emotional experiences together.

Professionals and Amateurs

When Marco and Tarox were appointed PvP leaders one evening in an important guild meeting with about forty participants, they immediately announced that things would be getting tougher now. 'What we want to do is to train you', they explained, making it clear that they would soon be abandoning the conversational tone in the guild's voice channel. Among other things, they wanted to teach us how to fulfil our particular tasks effectively, how to move as a group, how to push forward in a battle, how to avoid enemy attacks if necessary, and so on. 'We're going to teach you these things until you puke', they added. There would be 'a lot of work' ahead, but through hard training we could accomplish greatness, they assured us.

I was surprised by their seriousness. To date, I had only ever played *TESO* PvP with a small group of players and had participated in big battles only as a bystander. Now that I had joined a large guild, I was to become part of a dozen-player PvP combat unit. All-decisive in PvP mode, the unit was one of many specialised, well-coordinated groups that train several times a week in preparation for capturing strategic points or castles of opposing factions. The discipline demanded by the PvP leaders and their understanding of our training as 'work' was supposed to enable our guild to be successful in PvP mode.

In other MMORPGs, the new leaders had coordinated game groups of several hundred players over several years. Here in *TESO*, they found themselves coaching a bunch of amateurs. One of the most important lessons, they told us in the meeting, is that in battle we act not in our own interest, but in the interest of the group. To set a good example, one leader promised to respond to the 'acute lack of healers' in our guild by raising 'one more healer for the good of the group'. He promised to invest several hundred hours of playtime to level-up a second avatar specialising in healing just to support the guild. 'You need to take off your blinders and start thinking for the group', they said. 'The more group skills we have, the longer the group will survive'. The same went for the points we would gain and the castles we would take. Effective team play also meant resisting to become what German players call *killgeil*, the urge to go for a kill whenever you have a chance. We were supposed to kill an opponent only if it benefitted the team. 'We're really going to nip your ego in the bud. This is about togetherness', they added. 'We're going to build a feeling of togetherness. ... We want to achieve this feeling of togetherness so that we can inspire people through PvP'.

I felt that the leaders' stated intention to create a feeling of togetherness stood in stark contrast to how they behaved. In one of the first training sessions, Tarox snapped at some players who logged in on a wrong game server, saying that they could visit other servers in their 'spare time'. With military-like discipline, they taught us new commands. At '3 ... 2 ... 1 ... Go!' everyone had to sprint off at the same time. Those who weren't fast enough were singled out – 'Too late! Too late! Too late!' Anyone who went too far ahead of the group was immediately warned. From now on, our voice channel was to be ruled by disciplined communication. Anyone who said anything not related to a fight or fooled around was immediately told to shut up. All we heard on the voice channel were orders from the leaders and strategic remarks from individual members. In a test run of our new strategy, we accidentally ran into an opponent's magic spell, which is marked by a red warning circle on the ground. Tarox was incensed: 'Look at the fucking ground! ... If there's a red circle with a flag in it, get out of there!'

Despite the tone, none of the participants complained. All of them seemed eager to meet the new standards set by the new leaders. Only gradually did I understand that most players saw the harsh tone and the military-style discipline as part of an overall positive process of professionalisation. They wanted to be part of the perfectly functioning unit that the new leadership was attempting to fashion out of a bunch of uncoordinated amateurs. Over many evenings, we met again and again to take part in the strenuous training.

All the training enabled us to extract more pleasure from playful virtual violence, as we celebrated ever greater successes and defeated entire opposing armies. The player Pandrael told me in his interview: 'Yes, it's just fun when you see that what you practice or what you learn, that you slowly learn to implement it, and of course you're happy that you didn't do it for nothing, but also have a visible result'. The professionalisation of the group intensified the pleasure of fighting together. At the same time, it allowed us to grow into an emotional community who took playful fighting in PvP *seriously*. This created new possibilities for emotional experience. The professionalisation made game-related skills and knowledge particularly meaningful, lending learning a specific emotional potential. As players improved, they began to consult websites with information on the game's possibilities, on the advantages and disadvantages of particular weapons, on the countless ways to support their team and gain an advantage over opponents. Even more important was the practical knowledge gained through personal experience. Take Julia, for instance. A very good healer, she told me that her skills are based on 'Learning by doing. . . . If I can't get something done, I look on the Internet: What do the others do? And then I try to optimise it for myself: What fits together and how can I do it better and how can I help the group better?' Tarox so valued the importance of practical knowledge that he lets his students make mistakes. 'Even if it's a bit mean', he explained, 'I like to let them run into a trap once in a while, during the exercises and stuff'.

The practices of teaching and learning in which we engaged are in principle the same as in other sports and gaming cultures, and they fulfil similar emotional functions. The acquisition of knowledge constitutes a continuous exchange of pride and recognition. When I asked Marco and Tarox whether they are proud of their students when their teaching efforts are successful, they answered affirmatively: 'You are extremely proud when you see: All right, you finally have someone who really accepts what you tell him, and through that really gets better and better from evening to evening, or from hour to hour'. Tarox added, 'This is exactly what pushes the feeling of togetherness in a group. When people go: "Hey, what they're telling me works"'. The guild leader Lela also described this process in detail: 'The more you do with each other and the more you share success and failure with each other and talk about them, the more you have the feeling of understanding and knowing the others better, even though it is a virtual world'.

As these examples show, the pleasure of fighting together and the pleasure of belonging to an emotional community are intertwined and complementary. The exercise and experience of playful virtual violence are the anchor points of the process, which can include talking about successes, expressing mutual affection, helping and protecting, boasting and praising, and communicating pride and recognition. In all these cases, playful virtual violence is the means to a highly cooperative pleasure through which players can share their emotional experiences with others.

5 Righteous Revenge and Transgressive Humour

'Become a Jedi Knight, and the Force will be with you'.[33] So reads the title of a large ad in a 1983 issue of *TeleMatch*. At the center of the ad is Luke Skywalker, who holds a lightsabre as if about to parry a blow. Underneath him is a monitor depicting the video game *Star Wars: Jedi Arena*. The message of the ad is clear: the video game is like the film and the player is its protagonist and hero. It is a promise that precisely describes the actual experience of some gamers. Painstar relayed to me the intense emotional experience of immersing himself in a game:

> What I've experienced in games ... has fascinated me much like a movie, because I could identify with the character, because I went on a journey with him and partly understand his actions, the decisions he made.... There are films that stir up feelings, sure. But the video game's potential to do that is greater and, during game play, much more intense.

While the general role of video game narratives has received much attention in game studies scholarship, it is important to note that players respond to narratives quite individually. In my observations, players do not follow narratives blindly; they oscillate between immersing themselves in and distancing themselves from the game. How is the emotional potential of virtual violence connected to these processes? How does playful virtual violence shape the narratives and emotional experiences of gaming and which specific facets emerge from their combination?

By way of approaching these questions, consider for a moment the meaning of physical violence in society. First and foremost, physical violence is a way to enforce power. As such, it stands in relationship to legal structures and culturally defined notions of common sense (Geertz, 1975) that deem its use justified in very specific circumstances. Physical violence is unjust when directed at the innocent – those who neither have violated the norms regulating violence nor possess the means to defend themselves. (This is why violence against women and children is so often considered taboo.)

Instances of unjust physical violence can elicit strong emotional experiences in those who witness or receive it. This is true for video game narratives as well

---

[33] Werden Sie ein Jedi-Ritter, und die Macht ist mit Ihnen! *TeleMatch*, 1983(6–7), 19. www .kultpower.de/archiv/heft_telematch_1983-04_seite18

as in everyday life. Since the 1980s, most single-player action games have adopted a narrative that starts with a dramatic moment of injustice. An example can be found in *Mass Effect* 3, the third part of a series known for its epic narratives. A reviewer describes the situation:

> We stare at the monitor in horror. 'They can't do that!' They, meaning the developers . . . And yet they do: in a dramatic cutscene, we watch the death of a character whom we came to know and love in *Mass Effect 1*, whom we protected from many a catastrophe in *Mass Effect 2*, and whom we met again in *Mass Effect 3* before a mutant brutally smashes [his body] against a wall . . . In this moment, we feel anger, sadness, pain – all while full of wonder for a game that can call up such strong emotions in us.[34]

Similar moments of unjust virtual violence occur in countless other action games. Again and again, characters lose their friends, comrades, lovers, or children through cruel acts, or they witness the torture or execution of innocent civilians by computer-controlled enemies. The atrocities prompt anger in the players, who side with the victims. As Robert C. Solomon (2007, 18) writes, anger is 'basically a judgement that one has been wronged or offended'. Unjust physical violence counts as an extreme form of injustice, one we are habituated to respond to at a visceral level. Players who immerse themselves in game narratives that contain such violence often experience intense moments of outrage and loss.

In Let's Play videos, gamers regularly express their strong aversion to adversaries that commit wrongful violence against their characters or allies. The aversion is most palpably manifest in the invective they hurl at opponents. Around 40 per cent of all Let's Play fight sequences I analysed contain one or more insults, though their frequency and severity can vary. For instance, fewer than 30 per cent of the fight sequences in Sarazar's LP videos for *Battlefield 3* contain insults, many fairly tame such as 'dirtbag', 'swine', 'arse', 'pack of terrorists', 'little terrorists', 'worm', and 'scoundrel'. By contrast, around 65 per cent of the fight sequences in Brammen's LP series for *Battlefield 4* contain insults, the majority of which are of an extremely vulgar variety: 'Chinese bastard', 'Chinese fucker', 'toad fucker', 'dog eater', 'wanker', 'shit eater', 'cocksucker', 'bitch', 'whore', or 'spaz motherfucker'. Whatever their frequency and intensity, however, insults demonstrate players' immersion in a game whose enemies assume the status of quasi-social beings. As an emotional practice, name-calling serves to communicate hatred of those who committed injustice. But in the context of video games it also signals a certain

---

[34] Matschijewsky, D. (6 March 2012). So beendet man ein Epos. Mass Effect 3 im Test. *Gamestar. de*.www.gamestar.de/spiele/mass-effect-3/test/mass_effect_3,45851,2565294.html

playfulness suspended at the junction between seriousness and nonseriousness. Players both know that it is just a game yet respond to virtual injustice as if it possessed its serious meaning.

Going hand in hand with the aversion to unjust violence is the desire to seek justice and punish perpetrators. Where laws exist, the task falls to the police and the courts. In the lawless worlds of video games – on a secluded island full of brutal cult members (*Tomb Raider*), in a fight against the army of a fanatical dictator (*Battlefield 4*) – players' avatars have to take matters into their own hands. The typical action game is set in a state of exception where extralegal retaliation against unjust violence is virtuous, desirable – and emotionally charged.

The phenomenon is akin to what communication scholar Jürgen Grimm (1998, 24) calls the 'Robespierre affect', the 'virtuous aggression' observed in television and movie audiences when watching depictions of physical violence that they regard as unjust. The violence offends viewers' sense of right and wrong, inciting in them fantasies of retaliation – a make-believe version of the fervour felt by Maximilien Robespierre and other revolutionaries as they carried out mass executions in response to the perceived crimes of the French aristocracy. 'The Robespierre affect', Grimm observes, 'is revenge in moral clothing' (1998, 24). In contrast to film and television audiences, however, gamers do not wait passively for the movie's hero to act. They can take immediate revenge through their avatars by slaying the evildoers in the game.

The communicative practices of Let's Play videos throw into relief the ways people respond to just virtual violence in the gaming community. First, the main driving force motivating players is not the desire to master games but the desire to right the wrongs that they experience there. In his *Battlefield 3* LP series, Sarazar swears to revenge the death of Jonathan Miller, a soldier and dedicated father who was brutally executed by terrorists. 'Now we're going to take care of the rest and finish the whole thing. Miller must be avenged!'[35] The Let's Player Gronkh, speaking about an opponent in *GTA V* who threatened his character's family, says that he 'definitely must bite the dust'.[36] Unjust violence not only motivates players to retaliate in kind; it also legitimises the violence they commit (Klimmt et al. 2006, 319–20). Typically, players do not point this out explicitly. It expresses itself in the matter-of-factness with which they seek to destroy their enemies. Another particularity of virtual violence is that it need not

---

[35] Sarazar (6 November 2011). Let's Play Battlefield 3 #012 [German] [Full-HD] – Durch die Nacht. Online video clip. 15:00–15:24. www.youtube.com/embed/vXVbQ8cUYA8?start=900&end=924

[36] Gronkh (26 December 2013). GTA V (GTA 5) [HD+] #102 – JESUS!! * Let's Play GTA 5 (GTA V). Online video clip. 5:055:15. www.youtube.com/embed/sPAzXiudrmY?start=305&end=315

be retaliatory to be perceived as just. At the end of his LPs for *Tomb Raider*, Sarazar criticises an element in the game he finds odd: Lara begins as a gentle young woman – she apologises to the deer she has to kill to save herself from starvation – but goes on to become a remorseless executioner with countless kills.[37] Some viewers have argued that Sarazar ignores an important distinction. As one writes, 'Yeah, okay, the deer didn't want to hurt her, so she apologised. All those people, they wanted to kill her ... why should you have compassion for them? It was just self-defence, seriously!' The intention of the enemy to commit unjust violence is enough to legitimise *preventative* violence. In some cases, preventative violence is mixed with retaliatory violence because antagonists have already killed friends or innocents and plan to do it again – this is why the player, as hero, must act.

Making Enemies

In multiplayer games, players often experience the stories as secondary to the action. One reason for this is that the constant communication between players distracts them from the narrative. The tension between just and unjust violence nevertheless remains crucial in at least some multiplayer games. Nowhere is this more evident than in the zombie survival game *DayZ*, where each avatar is only accorded a single life. When players start a new avatar, they spend hours, often days gathering the supplies necessary for survival and for defending themselves against computer-controlled zombies. When they die, they have to begin anew. Encounters with other players are often fraught, because it is impossible to know beforehand whether they will be friendly or whether they will kill your avatar and take your virtual possessions, undoing many hours of work. In a group interview, the player Kerby described his frustration: 'It's so annoying ... when you let someone live, or you meet someone, get along well at first, and yet he is one who, as soon as you turn around, shoots you ... in the back like a coward'. His buddy Milo added:

> Yes, I've had experiences like that! ... I once walked through [the city of] Electro and met a guy ... And he said [on the in-game voice channel]: 'Friendly, friendly, friendly!' ... And then we went into the fire station together ... [and he] looks at me, looks at my gun, looks at me again and suddenly he's hitting me with an axe and that's it. And that's when you get really angry.

---

[37] Sarazar (8 April 2013). Let's Play Tomb Raider #038 – Das Ende einer Monarchie [FINALE] [Full-HD] [German]. Online video clip. 16:20–16:35. www.youtube.com/embed/k4Zz99UADUU?start=980&end=995

On some game servers running a persistent virtual environment in which dozens of players can participate simultaneously, the same players are repeatedly present over several weeks (often every day) and can be identified by their names. Since the same players regularly attack each other, stab each other in the back, cheat, rob, or willingly destroy each other's vehicles, long-term hostilities develop. For example, the player Fenre told me about his 'deep hate' for the player Maxo. One time, Maxo, for no reason, blew up the vehicle in which Fenre had stored his possessions, destroying many hours of work. 'I was really pissed off then', Fenre said in our interview. 'What I wanted to do then ... I wanted to get the plane and fly it right into the middle of their camp while all the people [Maxo's group of players] were there'.

Not all players talk about 'hate', but most have an aversion to certain opposing players. Borke, for example, also despised Maxo and several of his team members because they always attacked first, even the weaker teams, and always took everyone's possessions. Worse, they were 'campers', cowardly players who lie in wait for others and shoot them in the back:

> I don't know why, but I really hate them, because they're the very people who on the third day [when his player group hadn't established itself on the server and was still very weak], we hadn't even been to the houses and we were dead within a second, because they were already ... probably camped outside our houses an hour or so before that and just waited until we opened the doors [so they could be robbed]. And so I thought to myself: 'Okay ... we don't need them as friends – enemies!'

The example demonstrates how the interpretation of physical violence as a drastic form of injustice can emotionally charge social interactions in multiplayer games, rendering individuals or entire groups declared enemies. My participant observation in *DayZ* shows that players' justifications for their own hostile acts are almost always based on tendentious assumptions. Most players participate in practices of robbing, assaulting, and killing other players but are good at finding reasons why their behaviours are right and those of others are wrong.

This process of constructing enmity has an emotional quality of its own: enmity as such is a powerful emotional experience, and it is precisely the intensity of 'hating' the enemy that many players seek. Having said that, all players agreed in their interviews that their hatred of opponents did not extend beyond the game. Players, like Wooshy, who ended up in an opponent's voice chat realised that 'they're just normal people'. Lela explained:

> I think it's perfectly normal that [if you've been attacked] you think, 'Oah, you bum!', right? Like, 'You ambushed me!' But I think that's completely

normal and that's part of the game. But as I said, we are all clear in our heads: the enemy in this sense is the other alliance [or a player of the other alliance] ... but the person who plays this enemy is not my enemy.

The ability to distinguish between opponents in the game and players outside the game keeps the enmity playful. Players focus their hostility on the former, which allows them to enjoy the dramatic intensity of the strong hatred they feel. As Pirou puts it, 'These are just the frictions between players ... which they seek to amplify somewhat ... to make the game more fun. ... It's not meant maliciously'.

Making enemies goes hand in hand with the emotional experiences of togetherness and cooperation discussed in Section 4. In many multiplayer games, allied players not only rush to help each other, but also take revenge when their teammates' avatars are harmed. In *TESO*, when a player avenges a friend by killing the opponent who defeated him, both player and friend are automatically informed by a message on the screen. Such in-game functions facilitate bragging about and showing gratitude for retribution. In *DayZ*, revenge is equally important, though it does not feature automatic notifications as in *TESO*. Clans in *DayZ* spend much time communicating via voice and text chats about the outrage they feel when an ally experiences injustice, which helps consolidate their emotional community.

When a clan is 'at war' with another group, everyone is expected to participate. For example, one of my *DayZ* clans – in a version of the game allowing players to build permanent settlements and establish a long-time presence – waged war against the RTR clan for several weeks. The enemy clan was clearly superior to us. They had killed our group and stolen our possessions more than once, and we came to see them as the bad guys – acting unfairly, always shooting first, attacking innocent players. To us, they were manifestly evil, while we were fair and just. Of course, there was no real evidence that our opponents were evil; they were simply superior to us. We nevertheless talked ourselves into a rage because we implicitly knew that our anger could multiply our pleasure if we managed to defeat the clan. Once, a teammate joined RTR's voice channel and told us they had been quite friendly. The rest of us deliberately ignored the remark and spoke instead of our hatred. The rare instances when one of us managed to kill an RTR were accompanied by jubilant celebration.

As a mediocre player, I was denied this pleasure until one day I unexpectedly came upon a large group of heavily armed RTR players who were looting an old castle. Since I was playing with a fresh avatar and had little to lose, I tried to infiltrate the group. (It is possible to do this without being noticed because so many avatars in *DayZ* look exactly the same.) When the group got in their cars to drive off, I jumped into the driver's seat of a vehicle, and though an RTR avatar was already on the passenger side, I was able to follow them without raising any suspicions. As I narrated my actions live on my group's voice channel, my clanmates listened with a mix of disbelief and amusement. None of us had managed to pull off anything like this before. I was eventually able to shoot the passenger with a gun from the trunk. In the ensuing chaos, I destroyed one car and killed two more from the clan. Loud laughter broke out as I told my team what happened. I was proud to have dealt significant damage to such a formidable opponent, and the feat earned me praise and recognition from my teammates, who were still talking about it days after the fight and even more than a year later in a reunion with some of the players.

As my example shows, vengeance through playful virtual violence can strengthen emotional solidarity among gaming group members, providing opportunities for displaying pride and showing recognition, for having experiences and sharing memories. The importance of a common enemy for group cohesion became especially clear once our war with RTR came to an abrupt end. Ten days after my encounter, we ambushed the RTR convoy with hand grenades, took out most of them in the crossfire, and finished off the fleeing players from a captured helicopter. Our voice channel erupted with cheers and exuberant laughter because we knew that we had hit them hard and that they would need much time to recover. 'Yes, men', Manu cheerfully observed. 'We gave them a proper penetration today. They were scared to death. I've never seen them shooting haphazardly into the sky like that'. We came back online the next day, eager to continue the fight, but no RTR players were on our server. We waited the whole evening, to no avail. We had hit our enemies so hard that they had decided either to change servers or stop playing altogether. We wandered through the woods listless, suddenly with nothing to do. One by one, we all went offline. It wasn't fun anymore. We returned again another day, but the other players and smaller groups on the server were no match for us. Worse still, they hadn't done us any wrong so attacking them wouldn't have been an act of pleasurable revenge. Eventually, our player group disbanded. It seems that our shared hatred of an enemy was what had held us together all along.

Feeling Rules and Their Transgression

The emotional experiences I have described in this Section so far are consistent with prevailing 'feeling rules', the cultural conventions that determine what we should feel or should not feel in a given situation. For the sociologist Arlie Russell Hochschild, feeling rules are standards used in emotional conversation to determine what is rightly owed and owing in the currency of feeling. Through them, we tell what is 'due' in each relation, each role. We pay tribute to each other in the currency of the managing act. In interaction we pay, overpay, underpay, play with paying, acknowledge our dues, pretend to pay, or acknowledge what is emotionally due another person. (Hochschild 2003, 18)

Feeling rules are what permit players to experience pleasure without shame when they inflict retaliatory violence on their enemies. But the pleasure that feeling rules regulate can also be activated when players violate the rules through deviant or aberrant practices. The first games in which players could assume the role of the bad guy appeared in the 1980s. Two playtesters of the 1987 adventure *Knight Orc* describe the experience in *Happy Computer Spielesonderheft*: 'Wow, that's an idea that's truly unusual: that you can assume the role of a mean, ugly, and foul-smelling orc instead of, as usual, acting as the brave champion, is top class'.[38] In 1994, some *Star Wars* fans, having played countless games on 'the light side of the Force', were happy that *TIE Fighter* gave them the chance to switch teams:

> The Darth Vader boys have been waiting for this. Finally, we can, alongside our idols, zip through the vastness of space and destroy one X-wing fighter after another – fantastic. I like the game concept tremendously, even though Skywalker fans will have their problems piloting TIE fighters ('I can't . . . gulp . . . shoot at an X-wing').[39]

The particular appeal of the game, practically identical to earlier *Star Wars* instalments, is that it allows players to do what they are otherwise forbidden from doing. The transgression arises not simply in performing an act regarded as unjust but also in enjoying its transgressiveness. The pleasure of emotional transgression constitutes its own type of experience.

The principle of transgression figures prominently in the action game *Grand Theft Auto*. In the first game of the series, released in 1997, players steer their avatars through a large city from a bird's-eye view as they commit crimes and climb the gangster career ladder. In a review of the game, Steffen Schamberger writes that *GTA* 'breaks all the laws' and makes 'the players into car thieves, kidnappers, and killers . . . That it's murderously good fun', he adds, 'may annoy old fogy moralisers'.[40] It is not only the life of crime that fascinates

---

[38] Schneider, B., & Locker, A. (1987). Knight Orc. *Happy Computer Spielesonderheft*, 4, 59. www.kultpower.de/archiv/heft_happycomputer_spielesonderheft-4_seite58

[39] Hengst, M., & Weitz, V. (1994). TIE Fighter. The Dark Side. *Power Play*, 1994(9). www.kultboy.com/index.php?site=t&id=2342

[40] Schamberger, S. (1998). Grand Theft Auto. *PC Joker*, 1998(2), 82. www.kultboy.com/index.php?site=t&id=5330

players, but also the opportunity to threaten or kill civilians and police officers. Schamberger cites the press release for the first game without a hint of moralising: 'Feel your blood pump the first time you hijack a school bus!' The review provides two screenshots in which the player's character guns down police officers and then stands idly by as the ambulance approaches. The caption reads: 'Typical mafia: first cause a bloodbath by killing the police ... and then calmly watch as firefighters and paramedics do the clean-up work'.

Over the following years, *GTA* became one of the most successful game series of all time. Once it introduced third-person and first-person perspectives in later instalments, it became a perfect example of an open-world game, in which players are free to explore the game environment, complete side missions and engage in everyday activities: work out, shop for clothes, visit a strip club, or go to the movies. But the exercise of playful virtual violence – against other gangsters, police offers, or bystanders – is by far the most common activity. In *GTA V*, the bystanders are the inhabitants of the virtual city of Los Santos, who simply lead their lives as they hang out on street corners, take walks, or go to work. The game by no means requires players to inflict violence on innocent bystanders, but it permits it – and many players are all too eager to overstep the boundaries of conventional feeling rules.

The most common example in *GTA V* is the hit-and-run. Much of the game is spent in cars (most of them stolen) while completing missions. Players often drive at breakneck speeds because they are under time pressure or are too impatient to obey traffic laws and end up killing many innocent people – pedestrians, bicyclists, motorcyclists, other drivers. For the Let's Player Gronkh, killing pedestrians on *GTA V* is a favourite pastime. In one episode, Gronkh feigns innocence whenever he runs over a pedestrian, declaring 'Oopsie!' or 'Sorry!' after each hit. Sarazar, who sits next to him, provides ironic commentary. Later in the episode, Gronkh runs over a motorcyclist (recommended example)[41] and both share a laugh. Sarazar, striking an outraged tone, declares, 'That's not politically correct ... That's quite politically incorrect, what you're doing here, sir'. Gronkh tells him that he's merely performing a government crash test as he steers his car over another motorcyclist.

The laughter of Gronkh and Sarazar is not the haughty ridicule of players who dominate an opponent. Its purpose as an emotional practice is to communicate their pleasure in committing unjust violence – and to render their behaviour transgressive in the first place. Gronkh's mock innocence mimics the very

---

[41] Gronkh (27 October 2013). GTA V (GTA 5) [HD+] #042 – PEDO-CLOWNS greifen an!! Let's Play GTA 5 (GTA V). Online video clip. 21:50–22:25. www.youtube.com/embed/9bdYzdRwY_A?start=1310&end=1345

feeling rules he violates. The joke lies in acting as if the death was accidental even though it was clearly intentional; in feigning guilt despite obvious enjoyment. Sarazar's reprimands serve a similar function. He apes the admonitory tone of someone shocked by Gronkh's actions before both players signal that they are in on the joke with boisterous laughter.

Such disparity – the difference between what people say and what people do – is often a source of humour. Many situations appear funny because they bring together elements that do not fit together. The notion of incongruity, the sociologist Giselinde Kuipers explains,

> implies a break with expectations. This break may be purely cognitive, but most humorous incongruities have a moral or social component to it. The mismatching often involves the transgression of social norms, or the breaking of established social patterns ... What is perceived as incongruous is always informed by culture-specific constructions of order ... This symbolic order entails cognitive schemas, but also provides a social and moral patterning of the world. Deviations of this order are often felt to be wrong, dangerous, repulsive, upsetting. However, as the anthropologist Mary Douglas showed, under specific circumstances incongruities evoke more positive responses. They can be seen as sacred, beautiful – or humorous. (Kuipers 2009, 221)

The 'transgression of social norms, or the breaking of social patterns' describes the behaviour of Gronkh and Sarazar. They break expected rules (intentionally running over bystanders) and display aberrant feelings (taking pleasure in killing innocents). Mary Douglas, the anthropologist whom Kuipers cites above, writes: 'A joke is a play upon form. It brings into relation disparate elements in such a way that one accepted pattern is challenged by the appearance of another which in some way was hidden in the first' (Douglas 1999, 150). Video game violence has a particular ability to generate humorous situations because it provides opportunities for just that kind of joking. Physical violence is subject to strict feeling rules that players can transgress and then distort by holding up a fun-house mirror to social norms. This is what Gronkh and Sarazar do when they ironically parrot the very feeling rules that they violate. By foregrounding the incongruity of the emotional experience, they create a joke that they and their audiences are meant to enjoy.

The *GTA* series is also known for the ability of players to go on rampages whenever they please. The more innocents they kill and cars they blow up, the more police officers or SWAT teams appear on the scene. This usually leads to a string of car chases and shoot-outs that ends with the death of the protagonist. In *GTA V*, this is of little consequence: the character always reawakens in front of a hospital short of some virtual money but with a clean police record.

To get a better sense of a *GTA* rampage, consider a Let's Play episode from Gronkh (recommended example).[42] Gronkh's avatar, Franklin, peacefully watches a crowd assembled in front of a large theatre modelled after a famous building in Los Angeles. Gronkh whistles innocently. 'Nice to see so many people out and about', he says, stifling a laugh as he selects a hand grenade from his weapons inventory. Still whistling, he prepares to lob the grenade into the crowd but accidentally drops it before he can do so. The people panic and scatter. Franklin pulls out a machine gun and shoots a group of people fleeing down the street. Screams can be heard; several fall to the ground dead. 'I'm not a good role model, kids!' Gronkh exclaims sarcastically. 'Don't do this at home! But the age limit is 18+, so you aren't watching this anyway'. As Franklin shoots a few people about to round the next block, police sirens can be heard. Franklin gets into his car and drives off. Gronkh lets out a satisfied sigh and says, 'I just wanted to . . . it simply had to be done'. When he notices a large contingent of police in pursuit, he expresses disbelief: 'But I didn't do anything! I'm innocent. I'm a victim of the media! I play violent video games. It's not my fault!' Gronkh somehow manages to escape without a dramatic shoot-out. The wanted level returns to zero, and he continues to play as if nothing happened.

Gronkh's emotional practices during the rampage are similar to those during his hit-and-runs. He laughs mischievously, feigns innocence, and alludes to the taboos he is in the process of breaking, including the long and heated debate about the link between school mass shootings and violent video games. His transgression is performative: not only does he kill many innocent people; he openly enjoys it while having a laugh or two.

Many of the 230,000 viewers who watched the episode seem to have enjoyed it as much as Gronkh did and offered words of encouragement:

> The main thing is that Gronkh has his rampage :D [grinning emoticon].
> Gronkh rampages for the first time. What's going on XD [grinning emoticon with laughing, closed eyes]
> Rampage ;) [laughing winking emoticon]
> Scarcely is Sarazar gone and Gronkh goes on a rampage :D.
> Way to begin with a rampage :D Killer :D.
> Kill everybody right from the start hahahaha.
> Hahahaha Gronkh, what an episode, blow everybody away :).
> gronkh that's what you are supposed to do in *GTA*, go on a rampage.[43]

---

42 Gronkh (3 November 2013). GTA V (GTA 5) [HD+] #049 – Anagramm: Komafaul * Let's Play GTA 5 (GTA V). Online video clip. 0:40–2:20. www.youtube.com/embed/tZr_lRXdCJI?start=40&end=140

43 Comments to Gronkh (3 November 2013). GTA V (GTA 5) [HD+] #049 – Anagramm: Komafaul * Let's Play GTA 5 (GTA V). Online video clip. 0:40–2:20. www.youtube.com/all_comments?v=tZr_lRXdCJI

The last comment is especially telling. In *GTA V*, going on rampage or running over pedestrians is not just possible; it's what one does. Even when the game's narrative or the specific missions do not require indiscriminate killing, the game culture of *GTA* encourages it. Viewers expect transgressive behaviour from *GTA* Let's Players because the practice of unjust violence is an integral part of the pleasure of playful virtual violence.

Of course, not all players of *GTA* or other action games feel the same way. A major challenge in ethnographic studies of transgression is that feeling rules are not static. They can change depending on individual experiences, opinions, and sociocultural contexts. For instance, the rampage described here was conducted by a German player killing innocent civilians with a black avatar at a well-known American landmark. For players with a different sociocultural background, the fact that the rampage was conducted with *GTA*'s only black protagonist may have specific implications for how they experience the scene and whether they find the transgression humorous. Here lies a clear limit of my work, whose exclusive focus on a small number of German players does not account for differences in the emotional experience of playful virtual violence. What it can do is explore some of the basic principles of emotional experience and the transgression of feeling rules.

6 Beyond Fun

The transgressive emotional experiences described in Section 5 repeatedly have moments in which the pleasurable suddenly becomes unpleasurable, in which doubt and feelings of guilt accompany the practice of playful virtual violence. In the examples I discuss, the players cloak the tension in humour. But in other situations, it can trigger disruptive, unpleasant experiences. This Section will take a look at the historical development of non-pleasurable experiences in gaming since the 1980s and consider how players handle them today.

At the beginning of the 1980s, video game journalists were divided about how to understand video game violence. The first home console games to feature killing of human characters had just appeared on the market. For some journalists, the games crossed the line. Helge Andersen, in a review of *Gangster Alley* (1984) under the headline 'Intolerable!', expressed his outrage that players are required to shoot gangsters and need only pay a fine if they accidentally kill a civilian.[44] 'And so that practice can start early', Andersen bristled, 'there's even a version for children!' He found the game so 'monstrous' that he appealed to the German firm that distributed it: 'Where is the voluntary self-control?

---

[44] An, H. (1983). Gangster Alley. Eine Unverschämtheit. *Telematch*, 1983(4–5), 20–1. www .kultpower.de/archiv/heft_telematch_1983-03_seite20

Does one have to go along with every macabre joke that is dished out from somewhere else [most likely a reference to the United States, where the game was developed]? Do we have a training program for terrorists on our hands?' The reviewer of the tank game *Battlezone*, the first-ever shooter from the first-person perspective of a tank, delivers a similar judgement:

> The fun stops here! ... *Battlezone* is not a game in the sense of what one ... understands by the definition of 'game'. It is not fun. The 'game' ... is paramilitary training. It seems that children are now supposed to learn ... what it means to take part in ... simulated warfare. And how nice it is! You can even earn points![45]

Though these and other reviewers were reluctant to embrace video game violence, many had to admit that they enjoyed playing action games. The same Helge Andersen who wrote the scathing critique of *Gangster Alley* noted in another review that shoot 'em ups 'if well-made can be a lot of fun'.[46] In the case of some games, reviewers were so mesmerised by the graphics that they looked past the violence. It is clear that playtesters from this period struggled with their own ambivalence. On the one hand, they were concerned that the virtual violence went too far, defying social norms and encouraging violent proclivities in players. On the other, they knew that virtual violence could be 'a lot of fun'. To justify the pleasure they experienced, they pointed to the abstract nature of the violent representations and argued that rational people can distinguish between game and reality. Ultimately, however, it came down to entertainment value. As long as a game was enjoyable enough, they saw its virtual violence as legitimate.

By the end of the 1980s, most playtesters stopped addressing their own ambivalence. The positive emotions they experienced were no longer despite the virtual violence of games but because of it. 'Roadblasters from Atari is one of those games you just have to have played', Martin Gaksch wrote in a review from 1988. 'It's a good feeling when you zoom over the street and knock over everything that stands in the way'.[47] The embrace of playful virtual violence paved the way for the overwhelmingly positive response to the rise of first-person shooters with immersive 3D graphics in the early 1990s. A milestone of this genre is *Doom* (1993), in which players can choose from a large array of weapons as they face off against hell-spawned demons. Although some reviews

---

[45] Battlezone: Hier hört der Spaß auf! *Telematch*, 1983(12), 27. www.kultpower.de/archiv/heft_te lematch_1983-07_seite26

[46] Andersen, H. (1983). Schnell, schneller, superschnell. *Telematch*, March 1983(4–5), 18-19. www.kultpower.de/archiv/heft_telematch_1983-03_seite18

[47] Gaksch, M., & Schneider, B. (1988). Roadblaster. *Power Play*, 1988(1), 109–10, p. 110. www .kultpower.de/archiv/heft_powerplay_1988-01_seite108

were critical, noting that the chainsaw was 'distasteful' and recommending that 'pacifists . . . steer clear of the game',[48] the vast majority gave DOOM a positive score for it's thrilling gameplay. In a review of the game for *Power Play*, Michael Hengst writes:

> The otherwise peaceful POWER PLAY editorial team has been transformed into a bloodthirsty pack: Knut 'Sexmachine' Gollert pounds a throng of zombies with his grenade launcher, Volker 'Chaingun' Weitz prefers to mow down his enemies with a chain gun, and Michael 'Brmm . . . brmm' Hengst hacks up his enemies into manageable pieces with a chainsaw. If we experience the baseness of human feeling in solo mode, we must jettison morals, ethics, or conscience entirely in 'deathmatch' [a multiplayer mode]. Without batting an eyelid, each shoots online at his best friends, and defends the location of a heavy weapon with brute force. But don't worry: after the murderous fight in *Doom*, we serial killers once again become peaceful buddies who wouldn't hurt a fly.[49]

In the mid 1990s, positive interpretations of virtual violence like this became common in gaming magazines, as reviewers began to respond to violence in video games with insouciance and humour. Taking pleasure in virtual violence had come to seem not only acceptable but downright positive.

By the beginning of the twenty-first century, a once deeply rooted feeling rule – the taboo of openly enjoying realistic war games – had fallen by the way side. Today, the fact that first-person shooters often take their inspiration from real wars both past and present bothers almost no one; on the contrary. In a review of the 2002 *Battlefield 1942*, Patrick Hartmann raves about the game's immerse experience: 'Finally, players are in the middle of battle instead of merely somewhere on the battlefield . . . The game's enormous battles', he writes, 'sometimes take on epic proportions and give the impression of playing along in a Hollywood film like *Saving Private Ryan*'.[50] When the very popular action game *Call of Duty: Modern Warfare* was released in 2007, players got to experience present-day conflicts involving Middle Eastern radicals and ultra-nationalists in Russia. Reviewers waxed rhapsodic. 'There is no other way to put it', Petra Schmitz writes, 'than to honestly say that we love the game and take part in this war because it's a good, no, fantastic pastime'.[51] Schmitz's

---

48 Rosshirt, R. (1994). Doom. 3D Action. *Play Time*, 1994(3), 110–11, p. 111. www.kultboy.com /index.php?site=t&id=355

49 Weitz, V., & Hengst, M. (1994). Doom. *Powerplay*, 1994(3), 28–9. www.kultboy.com/index.php ?site=t&id=4026

50 Hartmann, P. (1 October 2002). Grandioser Multiplayer-Shooter im 2. Weltkrieg. Battlefield 1942 im Test. *Gamestar.de*. www.gamestar.de/spiele/battlefield-1942/test/battle field_1942,37458,1338963.html

51 Schmitz, P. (14 November 2007). Großartig inszenierte, schnörkellose Dauer-Action. Call of Duty 4: Modern Warfare im Test. *Gamestar.de*. www.gamestar.de/spiele/call-of-duty-4-modern-warfare/test/call_of_duty_4_modern_warfare,43463,1476253.html

observation marks the culmination of a two-decades-long process of gradually accepting, legitimising, and enjoying the experience of video game violence. This does not mean that players' ambivalence has disappeared, however. Indeed, some more recent games have forced players to confront their ambivalence with new intensity.

Feeling Bad

We're standing in an elevator with multiple masked men armed with heavy machine guns. One speaks to us in an Eastern European accent: 'Remember, no Russian!' The lift's doors open, and we look into a crowded airport terminal. As we look around, panic breaks out. Shots are fired. People fall blood-soaked to the ground. The masked figures make their way slowly but resolutely through the terminal killing innocent people. No one survives.[52]

The passage is from a special report in *PC Games* describing the notorious 'no Russian' level from *Call of Duty: Modern Warfare 2* (2009), a first-person shooter in which terrorists intent on concealing their Russian nationality wreak havoc at a fictional airport in Moscow. Players of the German version must watch the massacre without participating – if they do, the mission fails – while the original US version allows them to participate in the killing. According to the publisher, Activision, the point of the massacre is to raise the game's dramatic stakes: 'The airport scene shows the viciousness and cold-bloodedness of a renegade Russian villain and his unit. The enemy actions show the urgency of the player's mission to stop him'.[53] For many of the playtesters, however, the 'No Russian' level breaks a crucial taboo. Daniel Matschikewsky, writing for *Gamestar* in 2009, comments on the scene: 'I'm shaken by the self-indulgence with which *Modern Warfare 2* shows the airport massacre. ... Despite how much fun I had with the rest of this enthralling, immersive game, the cheap sensationalism shocked me, and for me it devalues the whole game'.[54]

Matchikewsky's words express with full force the ambivalence that until then journalists writing about action games no longer talked about. They suggest that the brutal episode in *Modern Warfare 2* may not be pleasurable for everyone on account of the particular kind of virtual violence it depicts. In the past ten years,

---

[52] Schütz, F., Küchler, T., & Krauß, J. (13 November 2009). Call of Duty: Modern Warfare 2. *PCGames.de*. www.pcgames.de/Call-of-Duty-Modern-Warfare-2-PC-219515/Specials/Call-of-Duty-Modern-Warfare-2-699403/

[53] As cited here: www.pcgames.de/Call-of-Duty-Modern-Warfare-2-PC-219515/Specials/Call-of-Duty-Modern-Warfare-2-699403/

[54] Schmitz, P., & Matschijewsky, D. (10 November 2009). Packende Action, doofe Story. Call of Duty: Modern Warfare 2 im Test. *Gamestar.de*. www.gamestar.de/spiele/call-of-duty-modern-warfare-2/test/call_of_duty_modern_warfare_2,44634,2310440.html

a fair number of studies have examined the ethical questions that emerge from playing video games, with some focusing specifically on the 'No Russian' level (Mukherjee 2011; Schott 2016, 197–214; Sicart 2012). But their inquiries into the ambivalence players feel have only been peripheral. Let's Play videos provide many examples for fleshing out players' unpleasurable emotional experiences. Based on my study of Let's Play videos, I have identified three kinds.

The first is shock at the detail and explicitness of audio-visual representations of physical violence. For example, Gronkh's avatar in the horror action game *Outlast* is taken prisoner, and the player is forced to watch from a first-person perspective as a mad scientist cuts off each of the protagonist's ring fingers.[55] The avatar screams, whimpers, cries, and vomits on the floor. Gronkh, visible in the facecam, stares aghast at the screen, looks up at the camera, and then, after a long pause, lets out a laugh. The laugh is a response to the incongruity of the situation, yet he does not enjoy the experience. 'Man, what kind of game is this? What have I done to myself here? Man . . . you can't be serious. Who programs stuff like this?'

The second kind of unpleasurable experience is the empathy players feel for computer-controlled characters subjected to virtual violence. While playing *Battlefield 4*, the Let's Player Brammen searches a sinking freighter in a squad of elite soldiers and discovers several brothers-at-arms trapped in rising water under metal grates (recommended example).[56] The commander, seeing the grates are welded in place, presses the others to continue their mission, on whose success the lives of many others depend. 'Man, that's really crazy, if you just simply . . . ', Brammen says, before he is interrupted by the voice of one of the trapped soldiers: 'Please don't let us die down here!' As he reluctantly moves his avatar into the next room, one calls out in desperation: 'No, please! Tell my mom! Tell my mom! I can't die like this! Not in this hole!' Brammen is shaken. 'Man, no joke', he says, as the last gurgles of the drowning soldiers can be heard in the background. 'That . . . is sick. That is really sick'.

The third kind of unpleasurable emotion occurs when players inflict unjust virtual violence on others and either find no enjoyment in the break with social conventions or constantly swing between amusement and horror. The feeling is particularly frequent when playing Trevor, a psychopathic protagonist from

---

[55] Gronkh (15 September 2013). OUTLAST [HD+] #011 – Der Onkel Doktor ist daaaa! * Let's Play | Outlast. Online video clip. 7:50–9:15. www.youtube.com/embed/wtRhOC8fdnE?start=470&end=555

[56] PietSmiet (1 November 2013). BATTLEFIELD 4 SINGELPLAYER # 4 – USS Titan «» Let's Play Battlefield 4/BF4 | HD. Online video clip. 12:00–13:40. www.youtube.com/embed/nYQRyA6hG1A?start=720&end=820

GTA V. In one sequence, the Let's Player Piet begins a side mission with the character, who after a verbal altercation must kill as many 'rednecks' as possible within a set time frame.[57] Piet starts with the usual expressions of excitement, but as the corpses begin to pile up all around him, he enters another mode. 'Oh, we're sick bastards. Look how many people we're killing. This is freakier than normal, I have to say. I'm not used to this in *GTA*, not to this extreme'. Eventually, Pietsmiet completes his 'mission' with flying colours. He seems happy until he sees all the bodies: 'We've created a fucking mass grave'. His tone is briefly nonchalant. 'Yeah, that's how Trevor does it. That's how the wind blows here'. Then it becomes serious again. 'Sick ... just sick'. Finally, he laughs. 'I kinda like it. It's freaky though'.

Like the other two unpleasurable emotional experiences I identify, the third involves a moment in which the player takes a step back and considers the violence from a certain remove. Words like 'sick', 'shit', 'crass', 'abnormal', or 'freaky' signal the change in perspective. They indicate that, for the particular player, the game's representations of physical violence crossed the line. Of course, the exact location of the line differs from person to person. What one player finds shocking another may shrug off with a laugh. What is clear, however, is that feeling rules regarding physical violence continue to apply in video games, albeit in altered form. Breaking the rules can be fun, but it can also lead to horror and disgust. Developers typically try to limit unpleasurable experiences lest the game turn off potential players. For instance, while players of *GTA V* can indiscriminately kill bystanders, none of those bystanders are children, whose murder is the paradigm of innocent suffering and hence a potent taboo. More recently, however, game developers have pushed the limits of playful virtual violence and in some cases have intentionally sought to elicit feelings of guilt in players.

Guilt and Compassion

An example I would like to discuss at some length is *Spec Ops: The Line*, a third-person shooter developed in Germany. The player controls Captain Martin Walker, an elite solider who, in the company of two squadmates, makes his way through a sandstorm-ravaged Dubai teeming with renegade US military units and terrorists. Like other shooters, the game commences with pithy banter among the heroes and a few skirmishes with the bad guys before the real action begins. In his LP series of the game, Sarazar handles the

---

[57] PietSmiet (3 October 2013). GTA 5 # 18 – Explosives Meth-Geschäft «» Let's Play Grand Theft Auto V | HD. Online video clip. 20:35–22:20. www.youtube.com/embed/Ag6YFjxxUGo?start=1235&end=1340

first few levels just as he does those in other action games – feeling stress, revelling in domination, enthralled by wow and bam effects. As the game progresses, however, he encounters something darker. It becomes impossible to distinguish between the good guys and the bad guys, making everyone a potential target. The soldiers stumble on the first mass grave. A voice on their radio indicates that people are being tortured. Later the squad comes across an entire enemy battalion and have the choice of using conventional weapons or white phosphorus shells from a mortar.[58] One of the soldiers reminds them that white phosphorus is a banned chemical weapon with devastating effects. Sarazar decides to use it anyway. Walker opens a laptop and activates a drone camera for guiding the shells to their targets. The first shells explode. Sarazar is thrilled. 'Bam!' 'Next, please!' 'Wham! They're definitely next! Bam!' As the drone's infrared camera pans across the battlefield, Sarazar spies a large group of people and thinks that they might be civilians held captive by the enemy. But by the time he notices, a shell has already exploded in their vicinity. Screams ring out. 'Holy shit!' Sarazar exclaims. 'Um . . . oh, that's how quickly friendly fire can happen, friends'. The three soldiers put away the mortar. 'We eliminated them to the man', comments Sarazar, his growing unease audible. Once the smoke has cleared, he beholds the full extent of the destruction. 'Oh dear, holy shit! . . . I wasn't supposed to kill the civilians. I've really been a bad, bad boy, contrary to my intentions'.

In the next episode, the squad advances through the devastated area they shelled (recommended example).[59] The ground is littered with mutilated soldiers, some still alive and crying in pain. 'Shit, man. The whole place is burning, and it's our fault', Sarazar remarks, and admits that he could have chosen differently. The dying scream for help. 'Fuck', Sarazar mutters despondently. 'Look at that, everybody's burning. And somehow it's all our fault because we had to mess around with the phosphorus mortar'. At one point, he tries to inject some humour into the situation. 'Looks like this guy was playing with grill charcoal', he says after coming across another charred body. But he realises that the joke is in poor taste in light of the nightmarish injuries wrought by the white phosphorus. A cutscene follows in which a dying soldier explains that they were only trying to help. Then the squad discovers an enclosed area full of dead civilians, their bodies horribly disfigured. Sarazar is clearly upset. 'Oh man . . .

---

[58] Sarazar (13 July 2012). Let's Play Spec Ops: The Line #009 – Die totale Zerstörung [Full-HD] [German]. Online video clip. 11:05–14:51. www.youtube.com/embed/Dwyp47GOlF0? start=665&end=891

[59] Sarazar (14.7.2012). Let's Play Spec Ops: The Line #010 – Schwere Entscheidungen [Full-HD] [German]. Online video clip. 00:00-4:55. www.youtube.com/embed/r9Vb5qdFfAo? start=0&end=295

I've got a really guilty conscience now. Oh man'. One squadmate is sickened at the sight and starts to argue with the other about who's to blame. Walker is silent but visibly distressed. He approaches the mangled body of a mother holding a young girl, her hand still covering the child's eyes. Sarazar is stunned by the graphicness of the image. 'How ... sick'. The cutscene eventually ends and as the soldiers push on, Sarazar summarises his impressions:

> Woah, friends, friends, friends. How heavy was that? That's probably one of the craziest scenes in the game so far. And we're probably responsible for it, we were messing around with the mortar, or rather, I was; that's on me. Point your finger at Sarazar: 'How could you!?' I'm happy that it's just a game. But it gives us a good look into ...

Enemy fire interrupts him mid-sentence. Amid the fighting, Sarazar manages to finish his thought: ' ... into the deadly reality of war!'

The white phosphorus scene in *Spec Ops: The Line* confronts players with something that most action games give a wide berth. What players first experience at a distance, mediated by the abstract images from the drone's infrared camera, is forced on them later in all its horrific detail. The situation is all the more shocking because the dead include innocent civilians as well as enemy soldiers. It should be noted that, while Sarazar thinks it was his choice to use white phosphorus, the game does not allow players to proceed to the next level without it. To be certain, a player who believes that he or she is responsible for the carnage might feel particularly bad afterward. But the 'reality of war' the game depicts here is so horrible that the purpose can be none other than to saddle players with guilt, regardless of whether they feel directly responsible or not. *Spec Ops: The Line* is the rare action game in which players must reckon with their active participation in virtual violence and emotionally process a side of war that is everything but gratifying and fun. Not surprisingly, the game failed to achieve financial success, and the developer has since returned to designing conventional action games.[60] But not all players shy away from the negative emotional experiences offered by the game; some believe that they make for a richer gaming experience. One viewer puts it in a nutshell: 'What I think was awesome about *Spec Ops* is that the game manages to give you guilty conscience'.[61]

---

[60] Peschke, A. (20 July 2014). Keine Käufer für kluge Spiele – Keine Chance für Spec Ops: The Line 2. *Gamestar.de*. www.gamestar.de/spiele/spec-ops-the-line/artikel/kein_geld_fuer_kluge_spiele,45733,3058059.html

[61] Comment to Sarazar (14 July 2012). Let's Play Spec Ops: The Line #010 – Schwere Entscheidungen [Full-HD] [German]. Online video clip. 00:00–4:55. www.youtube.com/all_comments?v=r9Vb5qdFfAo

Of course, the innocents who die in *Spec Ops: The Line* are computer-controlled digital representations. Real people do not suffer. In multiplayer games, real people are behind the avatars, but in conventional games such as *Counter-Strike* or *Battlefield 3* and *4*, death is not transgressive. Everyone you can kill wants to kill you. No one is innocent and there is no risk of collateral damage. An important exception is the zombie survival game *DayZ*, where players can decide if they want to work together against computer-controlled zombies or kill one another's avatars. As noted earlier, the avatars in *DayZ* have only one life, so every death is a dramatic event. I can attest to this from my own experience. I know how frustrating it can be to be killed. I also know the guilt of killing other avatars out of selfishness or for no good reason at all. Because death matters in the game and because some players had good intentions, I came to feel compassion for the misfortunes of others.

A number of players I interviewed shared my feelings. As the player Onkie told me, '*DayZ* was the first time . . . that I felt sorry for shooting someone'. He related an encounter in the game's fictional world. Having been killed by other players more than once, Onkie decided not to take any chances when he came across another avatar on an otherwise empty beach and fired his shotgun straightaway. As the avatar slowly bled out, it became clear that he was unarmed. Via text chat, Onkie apologised to the player, who was disappointed and frustrated. They decided that Onkie should give the avatar a quick death. The injured character slowly rose to his feet and saluted. Onkie described to me his reaction:

> This was just mean, you know? . . . Well, yeah, then I shot him (laughs). Yeah, now that was the first time that I was sorry that I really shot one of those guys like that, also, just the act of shooting this guy, that I had killed him like that [*exhales*]. Oh well, that was somewhat, you know: never before in a video game, that you . . . I don't know, that you thought about it [killing] at all. Usually it doesn't matter, you know?

The guilty conscience that Onkie and others I interviewed feel arises because they killed someone who was unarmed and did not intend to hurt them. In Onkie's case, he was also confronted with the emotional consequences of his actions while messaging with the other player. Of course, not all players would have responded the way Onkie did; some might have found it funny. But stories like his show us that feeling rules are no less strong in multiplayer games and follow the common sense intuition we have about actual physical violence: do not shoot unarmed people who mean you no harm. The possibility of experiencing the emotional consequences of one's actions is crucial here. Onkie's opponent is not only annoyed; he is sad. While opponents' frustration can strengthen pleasurable feelings of superiority, their sadness can evoke compassion, opening the door to discomfort as players confront unforeseen consequences of their virtual actions. Experiences with playful virtual violence are often balancing acts at the edges of feeling rules – and can quickly tip one way or another.

Conclusion

This Element has examined different emotional experiences with virtual violence in video games. By looking at emotional practices, I have provided an ethnographic catalogue of responses to virtual violence in gaming culture. My primary focus has been on pleasure and other positive emotional experiences, though I have also considered negative ones as well. Naturally, the study of emotional experiences is always susceptible to blind spots because some remain unseen and unspoken. But the advantage of emotional practice theory is that it avoids psychologising and moralising stances, which is important given the controversies surrounding the subject of pleasure in violent video games. If some of my interpretations feed those controversies, I hope at least that they have been cogent so as to create a basis for further discussion. Because the study was explorative, the emotional experiences it describes should be understood neither as final nor exhaustive. The point was to show how heterogeneous and complex the pleasures of virtual violence can be rather than reduce them to a single common denominator. The experiences have different levels of importance for different players and gaming situations. In most cases, they do not take place discretely or successively. Rather, the facets of emotions I describe in this Element are intertwined in many ways, both complementing and enriching one another in players' everyday gaming experiences.

By way of conclusion, I want to draw some further insights from emotional experiences related to violence in video games. Specifically, I want to consider what my work can tell us about the conflicts between players and their critics and about the study of playful virtual violence in general.

As mentioned in the Introduction, almost no one involved in discussions of video game violence has thought to ask why virtual violence seems to provide pleasure for millions of people. This is due in no small part to the moral panic that the topic has triggered (Kocurek 2012; Schott 2016, 33; Sørensen 2013). But the failure to ask this question has led to a simplified understanding of the phenomenon. Instead of considering the lived experiences of players, the discussion has focused on the games themselves, emphasising the graphicness of particular scenes or immoral aspects of their gameplay. The underlying assumption is that the players are more or less passive entities, always at risk of internalising the values of the video games they play.

I have shown that this assumption is deeply problematic. Of course, graphics and gameplay matter. But from an ethnographic perspective, gaming is a process comprising both the possibilities of the game and the players' specific ways of using them. I have repeatedly demonstrated that players' particular ways of engaging in playful virtual violence can enact very different kinds of emotional experiences. Though the study of emotional experiences can never be completely representative, my work indicates that the pleasure players take in virtual violence cannot be understood without paying particular attention to *how* video games are played by individuals. Accordingly, anyone who wants to understand the true impact of video game violence must consider both the games and the players' practices of playing them. Only then will it be possible to produce serious studies – and serious critiques – of video game violence. Only then will it be possible to really understand playful virtual violence in a given situation.

The primacy I place on player practices is not an attempt to evade the normative debates about video game violence. Rather, it is meant to provide a starting point for a more nuanced approach to those debates. Though my work does not take sides, it can contribute to the discussion in two basic ways.

First, by identifying the many ways in which emotional practices related to computer-mediated representations of physical violence produce pleasure or go beyond pleasure, the study demonstrates the unique emotional potential of playful virtual violence. What accounts for this uniqueness? The most important reason is video games' ability to let players interact with explicit representations that share the characteristics of physical violence without actually doing physical harm. For example, the changes wrought by damage or destruction often come in spectacular form – shots, slashes, explosions, etc. – which makes them an effective anchor point for aesthetic audio-visual experiences. At the same time, physical violence has various social meanings, chief among them as a means for subjugation and domination and hence as a tool to enact powerful emotions. Heinrich Popitz (1992) argues that potential for violence is a basic constant of human existence, even when its infliction is not explicit. In terms of practice theory, this means that we carry embodied knowledge about the consequences of violence, which is to say, we understand it on a deeply emotional level. Moreover, the complex system of rules that govern physical violence – when it is taboo, when it is permissible, when it is mandatory – are not only judicial and cultural but also emotional. The feelings it demands vary based on the situation, but they are always strong and polarising. All these factors are what makes physical violence into ·

what Trutz von Trotha (1997, 26) aptly calls a 'reality of feelings', one whose potential for producing emotional experience is practically boundless.

It is this potential of physical violence that has made its representation so common in popular culture – crime novels, action movies, and games like chess and cops and robbers – as well as in the visual arts, where depictions of violence range from ancient battles (for example, the *Alexander Mosaic*, ca. 100 BC), to sculptures of mythological violence (Benvenuto Cellini's *Perseus with the Head of Medusa*, 1545–54) to modern artworks (Roy Lichtenstein's *Whaam!*, 1963). From this perspective, video game violence is nothing more – and nothing less – than the logical continuation of a cultural phenomenon that has persisted for thousands of years. In some respects, it even surpasses previous forms. Its virtuality allows highly detailed representations of physical violence with which players can interact through avatars. Video game violence combines the strengths of film, literature, visual arts, and physically active games. More still, the virtuality permits players to communicate to each other at a meta level that the violence is not serious (Bateson 2006). By being playful, virtual violence can be a constitutive element of competition, togetherness, drama, transgression, ambivalence, and critical self-reflection. Through the interwovenness of these potentials, playful virtual violence is an especially effective way to enact the emotional potential of physical violence for the purposes of pleasure. This also helps explain, if not universally and deterministically, what gives people so much pleasure when experiencing video game violence. At the same time, it shows that playful virtual violence is not so easily replaceable – at least not when we assume that many people in our pleasure-seeking society are constantly on the lookout for intense emotional experiences.

The second way this Element contributes to the discussion is by providing a lucid glimpse into the diversity of emotional experiences enacted through playful virtual violence. It is high time, I submit, that the debates about video game violence address the different emotional experiences of players in all their individual specificity. The same goes for the question regarding the potentially harmful effects of video games on their users. Those who pose the question need to acknowledge the existence of different practices and experiences instead of making blanket statements.

Ultimately, my work is meant to be a basis of and a call for more nuanced discussions of video game violence – among players as well as among critics. Gamers also tend to oversimplify the pleasures of virtual violence, particularly because they are loath to accept criticism for an activity they spend countless hours doing. It might be worth thinking about which emotional experiences they truly want to have with video game violence. Some may be more deserving of criticism than others, while certain potentials could be utilised more frequently. If the debates about playful virtual violence are to move forward, both gamers and non-gamers must reconsider their entrenched positions and habits of mind and learn to better understand the deeper issues. Much stands to be gained if they do.

References

Abu-Lughod, L., & Lutz, C. (1990a). Introduction: Emotion, Discourse, and the Politics of Everyday Life. In L. Abu-Lughod & C. Lutz, eds., *Language and the Politics of Emotion*, Cambridge, UK; New York; Paris: Cambridge University Press, pp. 1–23.

Abu-Lughod, L., & Lutz, C. eds. (1990b). *Language and the Politics of Emotion*, Cambridge, UK; New York; Paris: Cambridge University Press.

Bareither, C. (2016). *Gewalt im Computerspiel: Facetten eines Vergnügens*. Bielefeld: transcript.

Bateson, G. (2006). A Theory of Play and Fantasy. In K. Salen & K. Zimmerman, eds., *The Game Design Reader: A Rules of Play Anthology*, Cambridge, MA; London: MIT Press, pp. 314–28.

Beck, S. (1997). *Umgang mit Technik: Kulturelle Praxen und kulturwissenschaftliche Forschungskonzepte*, Vol. 4, Berlin: Akademie Verlag.

Boellstorff, T. (2008). *Coming of Age in Second Life: An Anthropologist Explores the Virtually Human*, Princeton: Princeton University Press.

Boellstorff, T., Nardi, B., Pearce, C., & Taylor, T. L. (2012). *Ethnography and Virtual Worlds: A Handbook of Method*, Princeton: Princeton Univ. Press.

Borutta, M., & Verheyen, N. (2010). Vulkanier und Choleriker? Männlichkeit und Emotion in der deutschen Geschichte 1800–2000. In M. Borutta & N. Verheyen, eds., *Die Präsenz der Gefühle: Männlichkeit und Emotion in der Moderne*, Vol. 2, Bielefeld: transcript, pp. 11–39.

Breidenstein, G., Hirschauer, S., Kalthoff, H., & Nieswand, B. (2015). *Ethnografie: Die Praxis der Feldforschung*, 2nd ed., Konstanz; München: UVK Verlagsgesellschaft.

Brenneis, D. (1990). Shared and Solitary Sentiments: The Discourse of Friendship, Play and Anger in Bhatgaon. In L. Abu-Lughod & C. Lutz, eds., *Language and the Politics of Emotion*, Cambridge, UK; New York; Paris: Cambridge University Press, pp. 113–25.

Brey, P. (2000). Technology and Embodiment in Ihde and Merleau-Ponty. In C. Mitcham, ed., *Metaphysics, Epistemology, and Technology*, Amsterdam: JAI, pp. 45–58.

Brey, P. (2014). The Physical and Social Reality of Virtual Worlds. In M. Grimshaw, ed., *The Oxford Handbook of Virtuality*, Oxford: Oxford University Press, pp. 42–54.

Collins, R. (2008). *Violence: A Micro-Sociological Theory*, Princeton: Princeton University Press.

Dewey, J. (1980). *Art as Experience*, New York: Perigee Books.

Douglas, M. (1999). Jokes. In *Implicit Meanings. Selected Essays in Anthropology*, 2nd ed., London; New York: Routledge, pp. 146–63.

Ekman, P. (1972). Universals and Cultural Differences in Facial Expressions of Emotion. In J. K. Cole, ed., *Nebraska Symposium on Motivation 1971*, Lincoln: University of Nebraska Press, pp. 207–2.

Elias, N. (1986). Introduction. In N. Elias & E. Dunning, *Quest for Excitement: Sport and Leisure in the Civilizing Process*, Oxford, NY: Basil Blackwell, pp. 19–62.

Elias, N., & Dunning, E. (1986). *Quest for Excitement: Sport and Leisure in the Civilizing Process*, Oxford, New York: Basil Blackwell.

Emerson, R. M., Fretz, R. I., & Shaw, L. L. (2011). *Writing Ethnographic Fieldnotes*, 2nd ed., Chicago; London: The University of Chicago Press.

Fiske, J. (1989). *Understanding Popular Culture*, London: Unwin Hyman.

Geertz, C. (1975). Common Sense as a Cultural System. *The Antioch Review*, **33**(1), 5–26.

Grimm, J. (1998). Der Robespierre-Affekt: Nichtimitative Wege filmischer Aggressionsvermittlung. *Tv Diskurs*, **5**(2), 18–20.

Heidegger, M. (2001). *Being and Time*, Oxford, UK; Cambridge, MA: Blackwell.

Hochschild, A. R. (1979). Emotion Work, Feeling Rules, and Social Structure. *The American Journal of Sociology*, **85**(3), 551–75.

Hochschild, A. R. (2003). *The Managed Heart: Commercialization of Human Feeling*, Berkeley: University of California Press.

Ihde, D. (1979). *Technics and Praxis*, Dordrecht; Boston; London: Reidel.

Ihde, D. (1990). *Technology and the Lifeworld: From Garden to Earth*, Bloomington: Indiana University Press.

Jahn-Sudmann, A., & Schröder, A. (2010). Überschreitungen im digitalen Spiel: Zur Faszination der ludischen Gewalt. In H. B. Heller, A. Krewani, & A. Schröder, eds., *Augenblick. Marburger Hefte zur Medienwissenschaft 46 (2010), Sonderheft: 'Killerspiele': Beiträge zur Ästhetik virtueller Gewalt*, Marburg: Schüren, pp. 18–35.

Jansz, J. (2005). The Emotional Appeal of Violent Video Games for Adolescent Males. *Communication Theory*, **15**(3), 219–41.

Juul, J., & Klevjer, R. (2016). Avatar. In K. B. Jensen, E. W. Rothenbuhler, J. D. Pooley, & R. T. Craig, eds., *The International Encyclopedia of Communication Theory and Philosophy*, Hoboken, NJ: John Wiley & Sons, pp. 1–5.

Klastrup, L. (2008). What Makes World of Warcraft a World? A Note on Death and Dying. In H. G. Corneliussen & J. W. Rettberg, eds., *Digital Culture, Play, and Identity*, Cambridge, MA; London: MIT Press, pp. 143–66.

Klevjer, R. (2006). *What Is the Avatar? Fiction and Embodiment in Avatar-Based Singleplayer Computer Games*, Bergen: University of Bergen.

Klevjer, R. (2018). It's Not the Violence, Stupid. *Game Studies: The International Journal of Computer Game Research*, **18**(1). http://gamestu dies.org/1801/articles/review_klevjer

Klimmt, C., Schmid, H., Nosper, A., Hartmann, T., & Vorderer, P. (2006). How Players Manage Moral Concerns to Make Video Game Violence Enjoyable. *Communications*, **31**(3), 309–28.

Kocurek, C. A. (2012). The Agony and the Exidy: A History of Video Game Violence and the Legacy of *Death Race*. *Game Studies: The International Journal of Computer Game Research*, **12**(1). http://gamestudies.org/1201/ articles/carly_kocurek

Kotthoff, H. (2006). Vorwort. In H. Kotthoff, ed., *Scherzkommunikation: Beiträge aus der empirischen Gesprächsforschung*, Radolfzell: Verlag für Gesprächsforschung, pp. 7–19.

Kuipers, G. (2009). Humor Styles and Symbolic Boundaries. *Journal of Literary Theory*, **3**(2), 219–40.

Lutz, C. A. (1988). *Unnatural Emotions: Everyday Sentiments on a Micronesian Atoll and Their Challenge to Western Theory*, Chicago: University of Chicago Press.

Maase, K. (2019). *Populärkulturforschung: Eine Einführung*, Bielefeld: transcript.

Merleau-Ponty, M. (2002). *Phenomenology of Perception: An Introduction*, London: Routledge.

Mukherjee, S. (2011). 'Follow Makarov's Lead?' Ethical Conflicts in Videogames and the Controversial 'No Russian' Level. In R. Inderst, ed., *Contact – Conflict – Combat: Zur Tradition des Konfliktes in digitalen Spielen*, Boisenburg: VWH, pp. 43–61.

Nardi, B. A. (2010). *My Life as a Night Elf Priest: An Anthropological Account of World of Warcraft*, Ann Arbor: University of Michigan Press.

Neitzel, B. (2008). Metacommunicative Circles. In S. Günzel, M. Liebe, & D. Mersch, eds.,*Conference Proceedings of the Philosophy of Computer Games 2008*, Vol. 01, Potsdam: Potsdam University Press, pp. 278–94.

Plamper, J. (2013). Vergangene Gefühle: Emotionen als historische Quellen. *Aus Politik Und Zeitgeschichte*, **63**(32–3), 12–9.

Popitz, H. (1992). *Phänomene der Macht*, 2nd ed., Tübingen: Mohr.

Reddy, W. M. (1997). Against Constructionism: The Historical Ethnography of Emotions. *Current Anthropology*, **38**(3), 327–51.

Reddy, W. M. (2001). *The Navigation of Feeling: A Framework for the History of Emotions*, Cambridge, UK; New York: Cambridge University Press.

Ritter, C., & Schönberger, K. (2017). 'Sweeping the Globe': Appropriating Global Media Content through Camera Phone Videos in Everyday Life. *Cultural Analysis*, 15(2), 58–81.

Rosenwein, B. (2006). *Emotional Communities in the Early Middle Ages*, Ithaca; London: Cornell University Press.

Scheer, M. (forthcoming). *Enthusiasm: Emotional Practices of Conviction in Modern Germany*, Oxford, UK: Oxford University Press.

Scheer, M. (2011). Welchen Nutzen hat die Feldforschung für eine Geschichte religiöser Gefühle? *Vokus*, 21(1–2), 65–77.

Scheer, M. (2012). Are Emotions a Kind of Practice (And Is That What Makes Them Have a History)? A Bourdieuian Approach to Understanding Emotion. *History and Theory*, 51, 193–220.

Scheer, M. (2016). Emotionspraktiken: Wie man über das Tun an die Gefühle herankommt. In M. Beitl & I. Schneider, eds., *Emotional Turn?! Europäisch ethnologische Zugänge zu Gefühlen & Gefühlswelten: Beiträge der 27. Österreichischen Volkskundetagung in Dornbirn vom 29. Mai – 1. Juni 2013*, Wien: Selbstverlag des Vereins für Volkskunde, pp. 15–36.

Schott, G. (2016). *Violent Games: Rules, Realism and Effect*, New York: Bloomsbury Academic.

Shields, S. A., Garner, D. N., Di Leone, B., & Hadley, A. M. (2006). Gender and Emotion. In J. E. Stets & J. H. Turner, eds., *Handbook of the Sociology of Emotions*, Boston, MA: Springer US, pp. 63–83.

Sicart, M. (2012). Digital Games as Ethical Technologies. In J. R. Sageng, H. Fossheim, & T. Mandt Larsen, eds., *The Philosophy of Computer Games*, Dordrecht et al.: Springer, pp. 101–24.

Sofsky, W. (2005). *Traktat über die Gewalt*, Vol. 16855, Frankfurt am Main: Fischer.

Solomon, R. C. (2007). *True to Our Feelings: What Our Emotions Are Really Telling Us*, Oxford: Oxford University Press.

Sørensen, E. (2013). Violent Computer Games in the German Press. *New Media & Society*, 15(6), 963–81.

Strauss, A. L., & Corbin, J. (1998). *Basics of Qualitative Research: Techniques and Procedures for Developing Grounded Theory*, 2nd ed., Thousand Oaks; London; New Delhi: Sage.

Tauschek, M. (2013). Zur Kultur des Wettbewerbs: Eine Einführung. In M. Tauschek, ed., *Kulturen des Wettbewerbs: Formationen kompetitiver Logiken*, Münster: Waxmann, pp. 7–36.

Taylor, T. L. (2012). *Raising the Stakes: E-sports and the Professionalization of Computer Gaming*, Cambridge, MA: MIT Press.

Tocci, J. (2008). 'You Are Dead. Continue?' Conflicts and Complements in Game Rules and Fiction. *Eludamos: Journal for Computer Game Culture*, **2**(2), 187–201.

Trotha, T. von. (1997). Zur Soziologie der Gewalt. In T. von Trotha, ed., *Soziologie der Gewalt*, Opladen: Westdeutscher Verlag, pp.9–56.

West, C., & Zimmerman, D. H. (1987). Doing Gender. *Gender & Society*, **1**(2), 125–51.

Wietschorke, J. (2014). Historische Kulturanalyse. In C. Bischoff, K. Oehme-Jüngling, & W. Leimgruber, eds., *Methoden der Kulturanthropologie*, Bern: UTB, pp. 160–76.

Acknowledgements

My thanks go to the players who opened themselves up to a perspective interested in playful virtual violence, and allowed me to be a part of their everyday lives; the German Academic Scholarship Foundation (*Studienstiftung*), which supported this work; and the many colleagues at the Institute of Historical and Cultural Anthropology at the University of Tübingen and the Institute for European Ethnology at the Humboldt University of Berlin. My heartfelt thanks go especially to both advisors of the original study for this book. Monique Scheer not only significantly developed the theory of emotional practices which was central to this study but, in many irreplaceable conversations, encouraged me to extend the theoretical framework, which has earned her my deepest respect and thanks. I must also thank Kaspar Maase in more ways than one: firstly, he advised this work with exceeding dedication and care; secondly, he cultivates a tradition of critical thinking that became central for my study; thirdly, he has through his own work and teaching contributed extensively to the establishment of the topical fields of popular culture and pleasure in the German-speaking research community, preparing the way for a generation of studies like this one.

    The preparation of the English manuscript would not have been possible without the work of Wesley Merkes, Philip Saunders and Dominic Bonfiglio. My thanks also go to the publisher *transcript*, which permitted the reuse of the German manuscript. The publication of this Element was financially supported by the Open Access Publication Fund of Humboldt University of Berlin. I would also like to thank Jan Plamper, as editor of the Cambridge Elements series *Histories of Emotions and the Senses*, and all reviewers of the English manuscript for their diligent guidance and important comments.

    Finally, I would like to thank my family, in particular my wife Sabine Wirth, who has guided this study from its beginning – critically reflecting on it as well as editing and proofreading – and to whom I owe not only many insights regarding the field of media studies but, above all, much motivation.

Cambridge Elements $\equiv$

Histories of Emotions and the Senses

Jan Plamper
Goldsmiths, University of London

Jan Plamper is Professor of History at Goldsmiths, University of London, where he teaches an MA seminar on the history of emotions. His publications include *The History of Emotions: An Introduction* (2015), a multidisciplinary volume on fear with contributors from neuroscience to horror film to the 1929 stock market crash, and articles on the sensory history of the Russian Revolution and the history of soldiers' fears in World War I. He has also authored *The Stalin Cult: A Study in the Alchemy of Power* (2012) and, in German, *The New We. Why Migration is No Problem: A Different History of the Germans* (2019).

About the Series

Born of the emotional and sensory "turns," Elements in Histories of Emotions and the Senses move one of the fastest-growing interdisciplinary fields forward. The series is aimed at scholars across the humanities, social sciences, and life sciences, embracing insights from a diverse range of disciplines, from neuroscience to art history and economics. Chronologically and regionally broad, encompassing global, transnational, and deep history, it concerns such topics as affect theory, intersensoriality, embodiment, human–animal relations, and distributed cognition.

Printed in the United States
by Baker & Taylor Publisher Services